SORRY, DOWNTOWN COLUMBUS IS CLOSED

BY

I. DAVID COHEN

ISBN 978-0-9796451-9-8

Printed in the United States of America

ACKNOWLEDGEMENTS

To my editor:

A special thanks to Jim Lifter, Jr. for his art design, formatting and editing of this book. Without his patience, diligence and creativity this project would have never been completed.

To my friends:

I want to express my thanks and gratitude to everyone I interviewed or who assisted me in producing this book. Without their input this book would not have been possible. Special thanks to Ireen Weinberg, Bette Young, Roseanne Rosen, and Saul Sokol.

The Golden Era of the 1940's, 1950's and 1960's was unique and downtown was an integral part of it. These same years were also "golden" for entertainment, insurance, real estate, medicine and the law.

Those of us born between 1910 and 1940 were able to experience one glorious period in the history of Columbus. As Malcolm Gladwell stated in his new book Outliers, "You are a product of the time you were born." Our time was fabulous.

ABOUT THE AUTHOR

I. David Cohen's previous books include: <u>Get What You Want</u>, <u>How I Got This Way</u> and the college textbook - <u>Prospect or Perish</u> published by The American College Press. His dozens of articles have appeared in Financial Journal Online and various national insurance publications. David lives in Columbus, Ohio and can be reached using the information below:

Contact Info:

        E-Mail: <u>rkcidc@aol.com</u>

        Phone: 614-861-0778

TABLE OF CONTENTS

DEDICATION 1

INTRODUCTION..5

THE DOWNTOWN EXPERIENCE..................................11

RESTAURANTS 15

NORTH & SOUTH HIGH STREET 37

EAST & WEST STATE STREET.....................................43

EAST & WEST BROAD STREET....................................47

EAST GAY STREET 53

ALL TIME "BEST" AWARDS...57

THE BEXLEY / EAST SIDE EXPERIENCE......................67

QUIZ TIME..73

RADIO & TELEVISION PERSONALITIES.....................79

MEMORIES 83

    MARTY ADLER ----------------------------- 87
    ARLINE & JERRY ALTMAN -------------- 89
    MIKE CALLIF ----------------------------- 91
    STEVE CARTWRIGHT -------------------- 93
    BARBARA DRUGAN--------------------- 95
    MARK FEINKNOPF----------------------- 97
    BARBARA FEURER ----------------------- 99
    VIC & ELAINE GOODMAN --------------- 101
    LOIS GREENBLOTT ---------------------- 103
    ALLEN GUNDERSHEIMER --------------- 105
    AL HARMON ------------------------------ 107
    BILL HARRISON ------------------------- 109
    TAD JEFFREY----------------------------- 111

NYE LARRIMER ------------------------------ 113
BOB LAZARUS ------------------------------ 115
DON LEVY ---------------------------------- 119
TOM LYNCH -------------------------------- 121
DAVID MADISON--------------------------- 123
NANCY & TERRY MEYER --------------- 125
DICK OMAN -------------------------------- 127
JIM PETROPOLOUS --------------------- 129
JERRY SAUNDERS----------------------- 131
JAY SCHOEDINGER --------------------- 133
JACK STEPHAN---------------------------- 135
ALAN & BOB WEILER ------------------- 137
WING YEE----------------------------------- 139

WHO COULD FORGET....................141

CREAM RISES TO THE TOP..............147

WHERE DO WE GO FROM HERE?...............151

FINAL QUIZ 155

SORRY, DOWNTOWN COLUMBUS IS CLOSED

WARNING

This book contains information relating to the 1940's, 1950's and 1960's in Columbus, Ohio. It will only have meaning and relevance to those individuals who have lived here most of their lives (age 15 and above) and were born prior to 1940.

I also suggest that if you qualify by age to read this book and you do not remember most of the locations, establishments or people, it may be time to take a magic memory pill.

You have been warned…..

DEDICATION

This book is dedicated to a great friend, golfer, businessman and family man. We "all" are so very lucky to have known and loved him.

Alfred W. Harmon
1925 - 2009

INTRODUCTION

A Long Time Ago

My mother, Fan Schilling Cohen was born in August, 1907, one year before Henry Ford introduced the Model T Ford. With her parents, Sarah and Rudolf, and her three brothers, Jack, Abe and Lou, they lived on the corner of Third and Main Street in downtown Columbus. My grandfather was a tailor and part time booking agent for traveling road shows. Mother still resides in her home in Bexley.

Mother attended the brand new Central High School and in 1926 was in the very first graduating class. Two notable classmates were Bill Kahn of Kahn's Jewelry and Bella Cabakoff, Les Wexner's mother. The movie stars at the time were Clara Bow, Rudolf Valentino and Douglas Fairbanks Sr. (silent movies of course) . Jack Dempsey was the heavyweight boxing champion of the world and Babe Ruth was setting home run records, while the Charleston was the dance of choice throughout Columbus and the country.

One years later (1927) the first talking movie was created – "The Jazz Singer" with Al Jolson. By the way, Al Jolson was a nephew of my paternal grandmother on my father's side of the family.

In 1929, Mom married my dad, Myron, and immediately joined him in a beautiful home in Baltimore, Ohio, a thriving metropolis of five hundred people. My dad's family owned the Fairfield Paper Company in Baltimore which manufactured corrugated boxes. The company was founded by my grandfather in the late 1890's.

In 1931 my brother Karl was born and in 1935, I appeared. We lived twenty-five miles from Columbus and I can imagine how much my mother missed the big city. We made many many trips to Columbus, especially to see my relatives and, of course, to visit downtown.

My very first recollecton of downtown was the time (age 6 or 7) when I needed glasses because I was having trouble reading the blackboard at school. We visited Harris Optical on East State Street, next to the Hartman Building. Afterwards we walked past the Ohio Theater to have lunch at Freckers. They had delicious sandwiches but their specialty was – ICE CREAM.

To me, downtown Columbus was the most exciting place I had ever visited. You do understand my frame of reference was Baltimore, Ohio, a town that had two grocery stores, one dime store, one bank and a drug store.

Once the war was over (1945) downtown Columbus exploded with activity. The soldiers came home, resurrected their careers, bought homes and purchased everything from clothes to cars. You could find all of these items plus anything else you needed downtown.

The Golden Era of Downtown began in 1945 and lasted until 1970.

This is our story…..

The author and his mother

The Fickle Finger of Getting Older

Recently Rita, my wife, and I were invited to a dinner party to celebrate a few wedding anniversaries and birthdays. The affair was held at the home of Barbara and Norman Feurer and the guests were Lois Greenblott and her fiancé Al Budin, Vic and Elaine Goodman, Terry and Nancy Meyer and Arline and Jerry Altman. It seems that we have all known each other since the earth cooled.

After the round of hors d'oevers and cocktails, we sat down for a wonderful dinner. It didn't take long for the "usual" to occur -- talking about the past – the good old days!! It has hit me that lately all people my age talk mostly about three things; their grandchildren, their health and days gone bye. As a matter of fact, if you try to change the subject and discuss something you are working on or some project you are developing, your listener will invariably say "sounds like that is an exciting idea, but at your age why don't you just relax and enjoy life." It seems once you have grey or little or no hair you are expected just to shut down and of course "Enjoy Life." What's that all about?

Now, back to our dinner party. We have all lived in Columbus forever and it didn't take long for the conversation to return to the game of "do you remember?" It happened that night, for the next three hours the topic was – Columbus Revisited – The Golden Age of Downtown Columbus. Each person recalled a fabulous story or experience they had regarding downtown. It was either a great meal at Kuennings, ice cream at Isaly's or buying clothes at Montaldo's.

On the way home I said to Rita, "Wouldn't it be great to write down what everyone had to say tonight so that these memories would not be forgotten?" She agreed and suggested I be the one to do the writing. She also said that I would need to do more research and talk with many more individuals so that I could catch the entire essence of what was going on in downtown Columbus during the late 40's, 50's and 60's.

What is to follow is what I have learned from the thirty people I interviewed plus additional research at the Columbus Public Library. Basically, I am a reporter. If any one disagrees with anything I have written, I'm truly sorry – it isn't my fault – you see I'm relying on information from some old, but wise, people.

THE DOWNTOWN EXPERIENCE

By June 1951 my dad had sold his box company and retired (age 46). We moved to Bexley, a suburb of Columbus. In 1952 I had completed my sophomore year at the Columbus Academy. I was looking for summer employment and my choices were either to work at a construction job as a laborer or work in retailing. I chose retailing.

Keen's Shoe Store, located just south of the Boston Store, downtown, ran an ad for a shoe salesman. Sounded good to me. I interviewed with the store managers, Harvey and Phyllis Vance who lived in Amanda, Ohio. Apparently, they liked me and the very next day I was their number one, and only, shoe salesman. I reported to work wearing a nice pair of khakis, white shirt and necktie which was the style of the day. I felt like a real retail executive.

Harvey and Phyllis taught me how to greet the female customers, either to ask their shoe size, or simply to sit them down and take proper shoe measurements. This was summertime and the main sellers were sandals. They were priced from $1.99 to $4.99. I earned $2.00 per hour plus a bonus on shoes that needed to be moved. Translation—get rid of the old inventory. If I did, I got a bonus. I loved that job and I owe a debt of gratitude to the Vances for giving me that opportunity. I learned a great deal about people and why they buy certain items. It has been invaluable to me to this day, some 57 years later.

Working downtown created a whole new world for me. Every morning I was given a half-hour break. I used that time to visit other stores downtown. In that part of town, I would walk through Madison's, The Union, the Boston Store, Mogols, Harry's Hat Store, Heaton Music Store, Dunhill's, Walker's and Pumphrey's. These stores were teeming with customers. I could feel the excitement.

Being downtown in those days of the 50's was like the Easter Parade on Fifth Avenue in New York City. The women wore hats and gloves and the men wore suits and ties. Many had straw hats as well. Everyone was "properly" dressed. I knew right away that selling shoes was far better than working on a construction job.

When I went to lunch Harvey and Phyllis usually asked me to bring back something for them. Because they didn't care what I brought them, I had the adventure of scoping out various eating establishments around the north end of High Street. The choice restaurants were: The Purple Cow, Wagon Wheel, Kuennings, the Continental, the coffee shop at Fort Hayes and Max's.

The entire summer of 1952 was incredible. I worked during the day. At night a group of us would travel to the Buckeye Lake Amusement Park. Was that a great summer, or what?

Birds-eye view of Buckeye Lake Amusement Park

During the next five summers I either worked downtown or was the athletic director of the Columbus Academy (Nelson Road) summer camp. I organized basketball, baseball and swimming activities for the children. The director was Mr. Charles Goodwin and the education director was Grace DeLeone.

I graduated from the Columbus Academy in 1954. On June 9, 1958 after graduating from Miami University I began my career as a life insurance agent in the Beggs building at 21 East State Street. For the next 40 years, my offices were essentially located near High Street in downtown Columbus.

Every major life insurance company in America was located right downtown. For example, MassMutual, New England Mutual and Mutual Benefit Life were all housed in the Buckeye Building at 42 East Gay Street. Today of course, they are long gone from downtown.

You have heard "my story". Now it's time to hear more important memories of the downtown scene, and later, from the people I interviewed.

Get ready – Get Set – GO!!

RESTAURANTS

The Scene

Bexley, Worthington, Dublin, Gahanna, Whitehall, Upper Arlington and Berwick during the mid 1950's were all bedroom communities. For the most part, 60 years later, they still remain bedroom communities.

In those former days....

> If you wanted to buy clothing, you went downtown.
>
> If you wanted a wonderful dining experience, you went downtown.
>
> If you wanted great entertainment, you went downtown.
>
> If you wanted legal advice, to buy insurance or real estate, you went downtown.

In other words, if it was happening, you went downtown to find it.

Let's explore and remember together those great restaurants, clothing and department stores, entertainment centers and specialty shops that made downtown what it was – The Place To Be!

Dinner Restaurants*

Without a doubt, Columbus had a huge and inviting variety of eating establishments in the area. Check out a list of some of the best of these, at least according to my humble opinion and old-age state of mind.

1. Kuenning's (3 locations)
2. Doersam's
3. Marzetti's
4. Tommy Hendrick's
5. Mill's
6. Seafood Bay
7. Jai-Lai
8. Meadowbrook
9. Ft. Hayes Hotel
10. The Top
11. Kahiki
12. Presutti's
13. The Clarmont
14. Mario's
15. Willard's
16. Reeb's
17. Lazarus (Chintz Room)
18. The Maramor
19. Benny Klein's
20. Max's
21. Ann-Ton's
22. Desert Inn
23. Stew Harrison's
24. Jong Mea
25. Ricardo's
26. T.A.T.
27. Tom's
28. Wyandotte Inn
29. Berwick Seafood Manor
30. Cedar/Hoff Gardens
31. Mohawk Grill
32. Earl Johnson's
33. Jay Van's
34. Hoover Restaurant
35. Florentine
36. Flamingo Bar and Restaurant
37. Corollo's
38. Top of the Center

*This list does not include private clubs.

On the other hand, if you were looking for an unequaled luncheon experience, you also had a number of fine establishments from which to choose.

1. Toddle House
2. Ranch
3. Forester's
4. Paoletti's (Formerly the Union restaurant)
5. Continental
6. Reeb's
7. The Dell
8. Knotty Pine
9. Queen Bee
10. Hayes
11. The Feed Bag
12. Curley's
13. Pewter Mug
14. Max's
15. Marzetti's
16. Lazarus
17. Benny Klein's
18. Jack and Benny's
19. Purple Cow
20. Mills Cafeteria
21. Kuenning's
22. Ringside
23. Dan's Drive-In
24. Rubino's
25. Eastmoor Drive-In
26. Town House
27. Merkle's Drive-In
28. Tom Thumb
29. Howard Johnson's
30. Dworkin's
31. Beverly Drive-In
32. Jack Horner's Drive-In
33. BBF

How lucky we were to have such great restaurants in Columbus, Ohio!

THE FOUR ALL-TIME BEST RESTAURANTS

Marzetti's

Almost without exception, Marzetti's restaurant has been recognized as the best all-time greatest eating experience in the history of Columbus, Ohio. Let me give you a little of its history.

Eighteen year old Teresa and husband Joseph Marzetti who immigrated to Columbus, Ohio from Florence, Italy, founded Marzetti's back in 1896. Their original location was on the Ohio State University campus and catered exclusively to OSU students.

Joseph passed away in 1911 and Teresa ran the business herself until she married Carl Schaufele in 1919. That same year they opened a second restaurant which became known for its salad dressings. In fact, many customers bought carryout orders of only the salad dressings. In the 1920's they created a ground beef and pasta casserole and named it "Johnny Marzetti," after Joseph's brother. That particular recipe is still a popular dish and is eaten by millions of people today.

In 1942, they moved the restaurant to downtown Columbus on East Gay Street and eventually settled at 16 East Broad St. By then, Marzetti's, was a four star restaurant, the demand for its dressings grew so strong that a portion of their kitchen was turned into a small-scale factory.

In 1947, the first product bottled for sale outside of the restaurant was Marzetti's Original Slaw Dressing. The person behind the slaw recipe was a young seventeen year old African-American woman named Katherine Hill. She remained with the company for seventy years. Carl Schaufele died in 1969. When Teresa died in 1972 the restaurant closed. Lancaster Colony bought the company, its fine salad dressings continue to be big sellers today. For more information just "Google" Marzetti's.

MARZETTI RESTAURANT • 16 EAST BROAD STREET • COLUMBUS, OHIO

23

Marzetti's Restaurant circa 1951

The Maramor

The Maramor was a restaurant located at 137 E. Broad St. It was founded by Mary Love. She combined part of her first name with the French word for "love" to create the restaurant's name. In 1945, the Sher family of Columbus bought the Maramor and, added their famous chocolates.

Danny Deeds became the over-all manager and Browne Pavey ran the gift shop. The gift shop became as famous as the restaurant. In fact, over the years, Bette Davis and Joan Crawford, Hollywood actresses, ordered many gifts from Browne Pavey. He had fabulous taste and never disappointed his customers.

Not only was The Maramor a great restaurant, but also a fabulous entertainment venue. I can vividly recall attending the nightclub act of Abby Lane who was Xavier Cugat's wife. She was absolutely gorgeous. As of this printing, she is alive and living in California.

As recounted by the Grumpy Gourmet, Doral Chenoweth, The Maramor was one of the first restaurants to be reviewed by Duncan Hines, before he was a cake mix. Apparently, the Maramor had garnered national attention. Unfortunately, the restaurant closed in 1973.

In a conversation with Nancy Meyer she gave me the following recipe for Chocolate Chiffon Pie, which was one of The Maramor's signature dessert dishes. Try it and I know you'll love it. It might even bring back some memories of other great desserts at The Maramor.

Chocolate Chiffon Pie

1 baked pie shell
1 tablespoon granulated gelatin
¼ cup cold water
½ cup boiling water
2 ounces bitter chocolate
4 egg yolks

6 tablespoons sugar
1 teaspoon vanilla
4 egg whites
¼ teaspoon salt
½ cup sugar + 2 tbsp

Dissolve gelatin in cold water. Pour boiling water over chocolate and place over low heat until chocolate is melted. Beat egg yolks slightly; combine with 6 tablespoons sugar and chocolate mixture. Cook together in double boiler for about 5 minutes or to a thick custard consistency. Remove from heat at once and beat until smooth. Let cool to lukewarm and add vanilla. Just as gelatin begins to set, beat with dover egg beater until smooth and creamy. Add to cooled custard, a small amount at a time, beating after each addition. Combine salt with egg whites and beat, gradually adding ½ cup plus 2 tablespoons sugar. Beat until stiff but not dry. Eggs should feel fluffy and moist and hold their shape easily. Fold gently into the chocolate custard. Handle gently so as not to knock any of the air cells from the beaten whites. Much of the success of your pie depends on how you handle this. Pile the filling into the baked pie crust lightly. Set in refrigerator to chill. Top with whipped cream just before serving.

The Jai Lai

The Jai Lai restaurant was founded in 1933 and flourished until 1996. The original location was 585-593 North High Street until its move to 1421 Olentangy River Road in 1954. The restaurant was founded by an interesting character, Jasper Wattering. His nickname was "Jap". Mr. Wattering was a vagabond who traveled the country jumping on and off trains. In those days he would have been called a "bum" or a "hobo".

For whatever reason, Jap had some cooking skills and along the way created a dish aptly called "Vagabond Stew". He landed in Columbus during the depression of the 1930's and met a woman who owned the Garden Theater (near 5th and High). She then sold the Garden and opened the Jai Lai.

The two of them operated the business for many years, until it later was eventually sold to Ted Girves, who previously was a fifty percent owner of the Brown Derby Restaurant. Ted was the first person you saw when you entered the restaurant. He became the "face" of the Jai Lai.

Some of the memorable delights of the Jai Lai were its Cesta salad, fabulous homemade rolls, herb butter and of course the best prime rib dinner in the Midwest. The restaurant could seat 750 people upstairs and an additional 450 downstairs. On a football Saturday 3000 would dine at the restaurant. The waiters at the Jai Lai were all experienced with 2 to 25 years of service.

Many of the busboys were fulltime medical and dental students. There are many physicians and dentists in practice today who earned extra dollars that enabled them to complete their educations. It's possible that the doctor who removed your gall bladder became a surgeon because he worked at the Jai Lai. Another great testament to another great restaurant.

Menu Items
December 12, 1961

Cup Fresh Garden Vegetable Soup $0.25

Milk fed Veal Bourguignon with Potato Pancakes $2.50

Roast Rib of Prime Native Beef, au jus $3.25

Sugar Cured Hickory Smoked Pork Chops $2.75

Fresh Apple or Peach Pie $0.30

Jai Lai Custard Éclair $0.45

This short list was taken from a menu that had 165 choices. These are just the highlights.

Source: William Harrison

The Kahiki

In 1954 Lee Henry and Bill Sapp opened the Top Steak House on East Main St. near Bexley. In 1957 they felt that Columbus was a good restaurant town, able to support another supper club. To make the new restaurant something different and unusual, the two men traveled extensively around the country gleaning ideas. After several trips and thousands of photographs, they realized the trend was to Polynesian restaurants. Throughout their travels, they failed to find one which wasn't successful, thus, the Kahiki was born.

The restaurant opened in February 1961. Sapp and Henry wanted to make the atmosphere authentic. They spent thousands of hours of research and planning on its design and construction. The person they chose to help them fulfill this dream was Coburn Morgan, a painter, designer, decorator and sculptor, who had a degree in electrical engineering and architecture.

From the beginning the Kahiki has been described as "something different". The structure was similar to amole meeting houses in New Guinea. The inverse curved roof, ranging from forty to sixty feet high, contains the designs found on many war canoes that purportedly repel evil spirits.

Other than the food, the drinks were the focal point of the restaurant. Rum, that magic word that brings to mind the adventurous seamen who sailed the tropics, was the basic ingredient for all of the drinks served at the Kahiki. The bars employed forty different types of rum in their drinks. Sandro Conti, bar manager, was born in San Salvador, raised in Nicaragua, and studied his rums in South America. "Sandro's Sin" was the specialty of the house, mainly because it was Sandro's own recipe.

Other Kahiki originals were: "Malayan Mist", "Blue Hurricane", "Instant Urge", "Head Hunter", "Jungle Fever", "Potent Passion", "Suffering Bastard" and "Smokey Eruption". Sandro's most intriguing drink was the "Polynesian Spell"

The Polynesian Spell

In a shaker with ice, mix:

> 1 ounce Grape Juice
> 1 ½ ounces dry Gin
> ¼ ounce Triple Sec
> ¼ ounce Peach Brandy
> ½ teaspoon Sugar
> Juice of ½ lemon

Shake and strain into a chilled champagne glass.

As Sandro once said – if it doesn't taste like the Kahiki's, just add a pinch of romance.

The various bars in the restaurant used an average of 1000 pineapples a month, and about 2000 bottles of the various types of rum. In one month more than 18,000 Polynesian drinks were sold. By the way, Polynesian drinks contain anywhere from one and one half ounces of rum in the "Derby Daiquiri" to five and one half ounces in the "Back Scratcher". The mystery drink, made to serve four people, contains eight ounces of rum and brandy. It's no wonder every one got drunk.

When it came to food, Phillip C.W. Chin was the executive chef. He was a graduate of Texas A&M in Mechanical Engineering. The Kahiki served exclusively U.S. Prime beef and steaks, and vegetables of the highest quality. Mahi-Mahi was flown in semi-weekly from Hawaii. The food was prepared in a line of kitchen equipment ranging from the most modern radar-range to the ancient Chinese kettles which in history, date back thousands of years. The proper use of this equipment enabled any item on the Polynesian menu to be prepared in less than four minutes. Showmanship was a large part of the experience at the Kahiki. A big deal was made of the preparation of the caesar salad (table side) by the maitre'd.

During the 1960's Columbus was blessed to have the Kenley Players at Veteran's Memorial. Many of their stars frequented the Kahiki. Some notable stars to be seen at the Kahiki were Gordon and Sheila MacRae, Julie Wilson, Jack Carson, Zsa Zsa Gabor, Hugh O'Brian, Betsy Palmer, Betty White, Maxie Rosenbloom, Arthur Godfrey and Gypsy Rose Lee. Unfortunately, the Kahiki went out of business. Great memories of a great restaurant and bar remain to this day. One of a kind, never to be seen again.

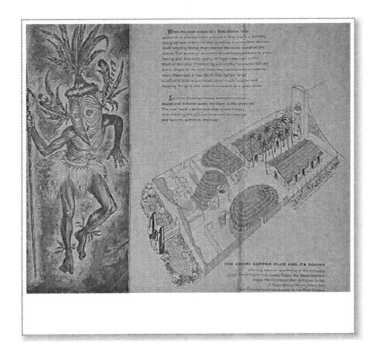

Some Sample Menu and Drink Prices from The Kahiki

Appetizers

Jumbo Gulf Shrimp Cocktail Supreme	$0.95
Chilled Tomato Juice	$0.25
Hawaiian Barbeque Back Ribs	$1.95

Salads

Tossed Green Salad Kahiki	$0.75
Roquefort Cheese (dry or cream)	$0.25

Entrees

Grilled Ham Steak Hong Kong	$2.50
Butter-steamed Red Snapper	$2.50
Almond Chicken China	$2.65
Pressed Duck Mandarin	$2.65
Sweet and Sour Pork	$2.25
Pork and Shrimp Foo Yung	$1.95
Lobster Cantonese	$3.75
Shrimp Royal Cashew	$2.95

Desserts

Fresh Frosted Pineapple	$1.50
Tangerine Sherbet	$0.35
Rum Cake Fiji (a la mode)	$0.75

Drinks

Head Hunter	$2.50	Hot Buttered Rum	$1.00
Blue Hurricane	$1.30	Coconut Kiss	$2.30
Malayan Mist	$1.50	Navy Grog	$1.90
Kahiki Pearl	$1.30	Jungle Fever	$1.30
Fog Cutter	$1.60	Tonga Tale	$1.60

There were thirty-six (36) drinks on the menu.

Much of the information regarding the Kahiki came from outside sources including an article entitled "Kahiki A Polynesian Adventure" that appeared in The Columbus Dispatch, September 24, 1961. They are credited with much appreciation.

No review of historic restaurants in Columbus is complete without a few "Best of…" lists and this book is no exception.

Best Signature Dishes.

Corned Beef Sandwich	Jack and Benny's
Seafood Platter	Marzetti's
Minestrone Soup	Marzetti's
Spaghetti	Marzetti's
Cake Ball	The Clarmont / Lazarus
Steak Sandwich	The Clarmont
Sticky Buns	The University Club
Coconut Cream Pie	The University Club
New England Clam Chowder	The University Club
Banana Cream Pie	The University Club / Benny Klein's
Chicken Salad	Lazarus
Cesta Salad	Jai Lai
French Dressing	Marzetti's
Broasted Chicken	Willard's
Texas Tommy	Feed Bag
Take Out Fried Chicken	Ranch
Kuenning Salad	Kuenning's
Celery Dressing	Lazarus
Wet Ribs	Jay Vans
Wet Roast Beef Sandwich	Reeb's
Liver and Onions	Reeb's / Blue Danube
Prime Rib	Jai Lai
Chiffon Pie	The Maramor
Pancakes	Feed Bag
Twin Burger	Eastmoor Drive-In
Eggs	Toddle House
Caesar Salad	Kahiki
Sweet breads	The Maramor
Turtle Soup	Reeb's
Floating Island	The Maramor
Ambrosia	The Maramor
Ice Cream	Isaly's/Frecker's /Johnson's

Founding Restaurants Still With Us Today
1945-1965

Year Founded	Restaurant
1945	The Florentine
1947	The Clarmont
1954	Dan's Drive-In
1954	The Top
1954	Rubino's
1956	Ding Ho
1960	Plank's
1964	J.P.'s Barbecue Ribs

How many times have you dined at these restaurants??

I don't know about you, but I'm glad they're still with us today.

NORTH AND SOUTH HIGH STREETS
1954–1955

Come with me now as we take a walk up and down High Street in 1954 and 1955. This will be a journey not only through time, but also through memory. Many of these places no longer physically exist, but no doubt they will remain forever in our hearts and minds as places we remember having distinct meaning in our lives.

Picture yourself standing in front of Lazarus on the northwest corner of Town and High. Are you with me? Our goal is to walk leisurely north to Spring Street. We'll stay on the west side of the street for now, but I will also point out those stores and establishments on the east side of the street.

Now that we have our bearings, let's start our journey north. As we proceed toward Broad Street we pass Baker's Shoes, Gray's Drugstore, Woolworth's, Peggy Ann Dress Shop, Forsythe Shoe Store and Neumode Hosiery. Across the street from Lazarus, at 150 North High Street is Monett Furriers and next door are the Sabre Lounge, Shaw's Jewelry Store, Morehouse Fashion, Gerstenfeld Women's Clothes and Hall and Steele.

Getting back to the west side of the street, we pass Morrow Nut House at 99 South High followed by S.S. Kresge, Spiegel's Fashions, H.L. Green, Walgreens, Jay and Steve's Women's Clothes. We now have arrived at 41 South High St., The Neil House Hotel. Continuing our walk we pass by Jack Lord Men's Furnishings, Mary Lee Candies, Jarman Shoes and The Travel Shop Luggage at 19 South High St. Looking across the street we see the Ohio Statehouse in all of its white stone glory.

Finally, we arrive at 17 South High, the Huntington Bank Building. Tenants include MetLife, Northwestern Mutual, Sweney-Cartwright, T.N. Meeks & Co. attorney Abe Gertner, Prudential Insurance, Gates McDonald, actuaries and the Porter Wright law firm.

At 15 South High we see Roger's Jewelers followed by Flagg Brothers Shoe Store, the Wagon Wheel Restaurant, National Peanut Corp. and on the southwest corner of Broad and High the Adam Hat Store.

Our journey continues on the northwest corner of Broad and High – at 1 North High is Gray Drug Store, at 5 N. High is Russ Bee Men's Clothing and finally at 9 N. High we reach the Deshler-Wallick Hotel. Before we arrive at Gay Street we pass Dunhills, Kuennings, Hanover Shoes, National Shirt Shop, Walkers, WBNS radio, Richmond's, Nunn-Bush shoe store and on the southwest corner of Gay and Broad is the Ohio National Bank.

On the east side of the street we have passed Roy's Jewelers, Benny Klein's, Rick's Jewelers, John H. Pumphrey Co., Standard Savings and Loan, Kahn's Jewelers, Thompson's Restaurant, Budd & Co. Jewelers, Howald Furniture Company, Stone's Grill and Green's Men's Furnishings. Finally, near Gay Street, was Heaton's Music Store at 50 N. High Street.

Continuing on the west side of the street, at Gay and High we can visit W.T. Grant, Kinney Shoes, Holly Shop Women's Clothes, S.S. Kresge Co. at 85 N. High and a second S.S. Kresge store at 95 N. High. Woolworth's is located at 105 N. High and H.L. Green at 113.

Across the street we passed Madison's at 72 North High, followed by Harrington Jewelers, Bradford Hush Women's Clothes, Singer Sewing Machines and Kay's Jewelers at 98 North High. At 100 North High we can visit McClelland's book store, Taft's Women's Clothiers at 104 or J.C. Penney at 106 North High. Neumode Hosiery and Hall & Steele will take us to Long and High.

On the corner of Long and High we see, The Union, a white brick, six floor department store. Up the street we pass Tom McCann Shoes and at 149 N. High, Hardy Shoes. We then see Sherman's Clothing Store and The Clock restaurant at 161 N. High. Walkover Shoes is located at 163 and the Shoe Box is 169. Further up the street we can stop for a bite of lunch or dinner at the Seafood Bay.

On the east side at Long and High is the High-Long Cigar Store followed by the Deluxe Hosiery Shop and Nisby Shoe Co. – Schiff's Shoes address is 142 and the Boston Store is located at 150 North High. Keen's shoe store and Mogol's Men's Shop are at Spring and High.

Downtown on High Street certainly had a huge variety of clothing, eating, jewelry and other business establishments. Downtown High Street was magical!

EAST & WEST STATE STREETS

East State Street

Let's continue our journey and focus on East State Street. Starting at 3 East State and walking to Third Street we will pass…Gary's Jewelers, Small Fry Restaurant, Harry J. Rook, Necchi-Elna Sewing Machines, Beggs Building, Kathryn S. Bell Corsetiere, Russel's Shoe Store, Loew's Ohio Theater, Elbow Restaurant, Isaly's, Wendt-Bristol Drugstore, 1st Federal Savings & Loan, Grand Theater Building, RKO Grand Theater, Harris Jewelers, Don McCallister Camera, and finally the Hartman Theater.

West State Street

The establishments and addresses on West State Street to Front Street.

Establishment	Address
State-High Building	5
Anderson's Grill	11
Bismark Grill Restaurant	13
George's Dye Shop	15
Morris Parish, Tailor	15 ½
Coral Reef Restaurant	17
Ross Cleaners	21

EAST & WEST BROAD STREETS

East Broad Street

Located at 6 East Broad Street was the great Jack and Benny's next to the 8 East Broad Street building. The real estate firms of Preston Cooke and Harry R. Roth were tenants plus a number of prominent attorneys:

- § Isaac and Postewaite
- § Alex Dombey
- § James W. Huffman
- § Lewis Bascon
- § John Chester
- § Harry Nester
- § Carlyle Huntington

From 10 East Broad to 72 East Broad the following businesses and buildings served our downtown needs:

- § Brunson Bank and Trust Company (10 East Broad)
- § Marzetti's (16 East Broad)
- § City National Bank (20 East Broad)
- § Outlook Building (44 East Broad)
- § Roy B. Smurr Jewelry (46 East Broad)
- § Camera Shop (48 East Broad)
- § Railroad Savings & Loan (60 East Broad)
- § Ohio State Journal Building (62 East Broad)
- § State Savings & Loan (66 East Broad)
- § Smoker's Haven (72 East Broad)

Between 3rd and 4th Streets, on the same side of the street we would pass by:

- § Menor Shoe Store (100 East Broad)
- § Harris Optical (106 East Broad)
- § Summers and Son (114 East Broad)
- § Athletic Club (136 East Broad)
- § Jane Rumberger (146 East Broad)
- § Doyle Shop (148 East Broad)
- § Sabback's (154 East Broad)

Between 3rd and 4th Streets, on the South side of the street we would pass:

- § Milgrim's (135 East Broad)
- § Maramor (137 East Broad)
- § Stark Altmaier (143 East Broad)

§   Montaldo's (145 East Broad)
§   The Columbus Club (181 East Broad)

West Broad Street

Located at 7 West Broad Street was Nathan's Gift Shop followed by the side entrance of the Deshler-Wallick Hotel. Across the street, Doersam's Restaurant was located at 11 West Broad next to the Wyandotte Building. The Broad Theater was at 45 West Broad which was next door to Albert Tyroler Optometrist. Across the street is the Palace Theater, attached to the Lincoln/Leveque Tower.

EAST GAY STREET

At 36-52 East Gay Street sits the Buckeye Federal Savings and Loan and office building. In the mid to late 1950's, many of the finest firms in the city called the Buckeye Building their business home, such as:

- The Galbreath Company
- New England Insurance Agency
- Richard Wetherbeee, Insurance
- Ohio Farmers Insurance
- Mass Mutual Insurance Agency
- Ohio Bell Telephone
- Mutual Benefit Insurance Agency
- John Hancock Insurance Agency

If you keep walking east you will pass Central Savings and Loan, Merrill Lynch, Pierce, Fenner and Beane.

At 50 East Gay is the Economy Savings and Loan and at 54 East Gay is the Columbus Hardware Store. At 56 is the Galbreath Mortgage Company and located at 64, Lawyers Title Corporation. At 70 and 80 East Gay you will see People's Savings Association and Pan Ohio Mortgage Company.

Directly across the street (south side) you will pass Nitschke Brothers and Diehl Office Supplies. Located at 51 East Gay is Dollar Federal and at 59 is Lyon & Healy record store. At 67 East Gay is located the famous Hayes Restaurant.

East Gay Street, in those days, was the "Wall Street" of Columbus, Ohio. Between High and Third Streets there were twenty financial establishments.

ALL-TIME "BEST" AWARDS
1945-1965

Men's Clothing Stores

Finalists:

- Lazarus
- The Union
- Harry J. Rook
- Thomas L. Carey
- Dunhill's
- Walker's
- John L. Pumphrey's
- Bonds

The Winner: *Harry J. Rook*

Women's Clothing Stores

Finalists:

- Madison's
- Lazarus
- Montaldo's
- Jane Rumberger
- The Fashion
- Milgrim's
- The Union
- Town & Country

The Winner: *Montaldo's*

Department Stores

Finalists:

- The Union
- Lazarus
- Morehouse-Martin's
- Luckoff's
- J.C. Penney
- The Fashion

The Winner: *Lazarus*

Music Stores

Finalists:

- Lyon & Healy
- Heaton's
- Summers and Son
- Van's Music
- William's Music Co

The Winner: *Lyon & Healy*

Social Clubs

Finalists:

- Athletic Club
- University Club
- The Columbus Club
- Columbus Maennenchor
- Knights of Columbus
- Columbus Country Club
- Scioto Country Club
- Winding Hollow Country Club

The Winner: *University Club*

Best Bars

Finalists:

- Marzetti's
- Maramor
- Clarmont
- Tom's
- Airport Inn
- Broad-Nel
- Benny Klein's
- Plank's
- Ringside
- Pewter Mug
- The Clock
- The Top
- Jai-Lai Cafe
- Athletic Club
- University Club
- Seneca Hotel
- Purple Jester
- Kahiki
- Leather Bottle
- Blue Danube
- Sabre Lounge

The Winners: *The Kahiki and The Top*

Best Office Building

Finalists:

- Beggs Building
- Huntington Bank Building
- Buckeye Building
- Atlas Building
- 8 E. Broad Building
- Brunson Building
- Chamber of Commerce
- Hartman Building
- Nitsche Building
- Wyandotte Building

The Winner: *The Buckeye Building*

Best Movie Theater

Finalists:

- Palace
- Ohio
- Grand
- Southern
- Broad
- Bexley Art Theater

The Winner: *Ohio Theater*

Best Nightlife

Finalists:

- Valley Dale
- Club Carolyn
- Dugout
- Roxy Club
- Lieb's Nite Club
- Kahiki
- Piano Bar – The Top
- Maramor
- Gaiety Burlesque
- Seneca Hotel
- Dessert Inn
- Playboy Club
- Ciro's
- The Gloria

The Winner: *Kahiki*

Best Men's Shoe Store

Finalists:

- Walker's
- Walk Over
- Nunn-Bush
- Lazarus
- Union
- Hanover Shoes
- Dunhill's
- Pumphrey's
- Hardy
- Gilbert's

The Winner: *Lazarus*

Best Hotel

Finalists:

- Ft. Hayes
- Deshler
- Neil House
- Chittenden
- Seneca
- Virginia
- Jefferson

The Winner: *Deshler*

Best Jewelry Store

Finalists:

- Argo & Lehne
- The Harrington Co.
- Hohenstine
- Kahn's
- Kay
- Rogers & Co.
- Eckstein's
- Lazarus
- The Diamond Cellar

The Winner: *Argo & Lehne*

Best Automobile Dealer

Finalists:

- George Byers and Sons
- Columbus Motor Car
- Packard Columbus
- Oty-McGee
- Saeger Buick
- F.E. Avery Co.
- Berlin-Wolf Olds
- Bobb Chevrolet

- Paul Davies Chevrolet
- McClure-Nesbitt
- Potter Gager
- Frazer-Kaiser
- Nash Motor Cars
- Winder's Chevrolet

The Winner: *Columbus Motor Car*

Best Drive-In

Finalists:

- Eastmoor
- Town House
- Van's
- Charbert's
- BBF
- Beverlee
- Green Gables
- Merkle's
- The Ranch

The Winner: *Town House*

Best Teenage Hangouts (East Side)

Finalists:

- Eastmoor Drive In
- Town House
- Glass Bowl
- Van's
- Tom's
- Airport Inn
- Rubino's
- Wentz Drug Store Soda Fountain
- White Castle
- Charbert's
- Massey's

64

- Dog Cemetery
- Merkle's Drive-In
- Norwood's
- Lois Garek's Basement

The Winner: *Eastmoor Drive-In*

Restaurant Owner/Manager

Finalists:

- Herman Loechler – University Club
- Carl Schaufele – Marzetti's
- Frank Kondos – The Clarmont
- Benny Klein – Benny Klein's
- Danny Deeds – Maramor
- Ruby Cohen – Rubino's
- Bill Sapp/Henry Lee – Kahiki/The Top
- Walter Ming/George Yee – Far East
- Browne Pavey – Gift Shop at The Maramor
- Clem Amarose – Ringside

The Winner: *Frank Kondros – The Clarmont*

Evening Dining

Finalists:

- The Maramor
- Marzetti's
- Presutti's
- Seafood Bay
- The Clarmont
- University Club
- Columbus Club
- Jai Lai
- Kahiki
- The Top

The Winner: *Marzetti's*

Luncheon Places

Finalists:

- Paoletti's
- University Club
- Reeb's
- Benny Klein's
- Marzetti's
- Lazarus
- Mill's Cafeteria
- Kuenning's

The Winner: *Paoletti's*

THE BEXLEY/EAST SIDE EXPERIENCE
1954–1955

Let's journey east on Main Street starting at Parkview Avenue. You would pass Willard's, Lex Mayer Chevrolet, White Castle, Bexley City Hall, The Feed Bag, The Drexel Theater, Ackerman Drugs, Capital University and Wentz Pharmacy. You have now arrived at the corner of Drexel and Main Streets.

Continuing east you pass Salt Brother's Realty, Colony Shop Women's Clothes, Bexley Record Shop, Little Tweed Shop, Connell's Flowers, the U.S. Post Office, Paul and Vic Hairdressers, Al Solove Kitchens, Cochran Pharmacy, Moling and Associates Detective Agency, 1st Federal Savings & Loan, Evans and Schwartz, Cookley Electric Co., Columbus Variety Shop, Bexley Fabrics and Curtains, Ross Cleaners, Bexley Art Theater, Sherwin-Williams Co., Mascari TV Sales (Former Glass Bowl). You have now arrived at 2500 East Main at the corner of Cassingham Road.

Located at 2501 East Main was the Bexley Pharmacy, followed by Bexley Appliance Service, Gregg Frame Co., Gift Shop, Paul's Foods, Bexley-Zettler Hardware Co., Fortner Bike and Lawn Mower Repair, Kroger, the Toddle House, and at the corner of Remington and Main - Ohio National Bank. By proceeding east you will pass Clifford's Sunoco Service, Rubino's, Main Street Plumbing, Bexley Cleaners, Roger Pharmacy, Johnson's Ice Cream, Bexley Camera, Wilhelmsen Pastries, and the Eskimo Queen and at Kenwick and Main Streets is the Far East restaurant.

Further out on East Main Street, not in Bexley, you could find the following restaurants and businesses:

Far East Restaurant (2801 E Main)

Van's Drive-in (2882 E Main)

The Top (2891 E Main)

Ciro's Lounge (2894 E Main)

Town House (2924 E Main)

Bexley Mercury Car Dealership (2935 E Main)

Eastmoor Pharmacy (2946 E Main)

Eastmoor Drive-in (2968 E Main)

Hoffman Gardens Restaurant (3015 E Main)

Question......How many of the establishments do you remember?

When we were kids, either we rode our bikes, walked or even drove our cars up and down Main Street from Parkview out to the hinterlands. In those days the hinterlands included Massey's (almost to Hamilton Road) and the Airport Inn at 5th and Hamilton. We also remember that on the way to the Airport Inn we had to stop at Tom's Restaurant and Bar. I'm sure the only beverage we had was a soft drink. The Feed Bag, White Castle, Town House, Van's, Merkle's and the Eastmoor Drive-in were our restaurants of choice. We didn't need Marzetti's, the Maramor or Kuennings, or The Top. Our parents dined there and we reluctantly followed, if ordered to do so.

People tell me that it's too bad all of these establishments are gone, except for The Top, but my response is – they may be gone, but the good news is that we are still here!

The Social Activities of a Typical Bexley Teenager During the 1950's

Breakfast

Feed Bag
Toddle House
Waffle House

Lunch

Feed Bag
Glass Bowl
Wentz Drug Store (Soda Fountain)
Eastmoor Drive-in
Town House
Van's Drive-in
Merkle's Drive-in
Miller's Drive-in
The Ranch
White Castle
BBF
Charbert's

Dinner

Reeb's
Willard's
Far East
Rubino's
The Top (with parents)
Eastmoor Drive-in
Town House Drive-in

White Castle
Massey's Pizza
Charbert's
Van's Drive-in
Miller's Drive-in
Ranch Drive-in

Nightly Entertainment

Airport Inn
Jay Van's
Club Caroline
Buckeye Lake
Tom's
Lois Garek's basement
Norwood Amusement Park

72

QUIZ TIME

1) Which women's clothing store was located at 146 East Broad Street?
   a. Madison's
   b. Montaldo's
   c. Jane Rumberger
   d. The Union

2) Which men's clothing store was located at 18 North High Street?
   a. Walker's
   b. J.H. Pumphrey
   c. Richmond Brothers
   d. Harry J. Rook

3) Which social club was located at 40 South 3rd Street?
   a. University Club
   b. Columbus Club
   c. Athletic Club
   d. Knights of Columbus

4) Which restaurant was located at 11 West Broad Street?
   a. Foerster's
   b. Blue Danube
   c. Doersam's
   d. Frecker's

5) Which hotel was located at 31 West Spring Street?
   a. Deshler
   b. Neil House
   c. Fort Hayes
   d. Jefferson

6) Which jewelry store was located at 37 South High Street?
   a. Roger's and Company
   b. Hohenstein
   c. Kahn's
   d. Argo and Lehne

7) Which automobile dealer was located at 288 East Long Street?
   a. Packard Columbus
   b. Columbus Cadillac
   c. F.F. Avery Company
   d. Paul Davis Chevrolet

8) Which department store was located at 124 South High Street?
   a. Lazarus
   b. J.C. Penney
   c. The Fashion
   d. Moby's

9) Which music store was located at 50 North High Street?
   a. Heaton's
   b. Summers & Son
   c. Van's
   d. Lyon and Healy

10) All of the following establishments were located on East State Street, except...
    a. Small Fry Restaurant
    b. Russel's Shoe Store
    c. Wendt-Bristol Drug Store
    d. RKO Grand Theater
    e. Hartman Theater
    f. Diehl Office Supplies

11) Which of the following restaurants were founded in the 1940's, 1950's or 1960's?
    a. Florentine
    b. Clarmont
    c. Queen Bee
    d. Rubino's
    e. Dan's Drive-in
    f. The Top
    g. Ding Ho
    h. Plank's Bier Garten
    i. J.P.'s Barbecue Ribs
    j. The Kahiki

12) Which downtown department store had both a grocery and a florist department?
    a. Lazarus
    b. The Union
    c. Moby's
    d. The Fashion

13) The owner of Rubino's was:
    a. Ruby Rubino
    b. Ruby Cohen
    c. Ruby Rosenthal
    d. Ruby Rudolph

14) Mayor M.E. Sensenbrenner was mayor of Columbus from 1954 until 1976. Prior to becoming mayor of Columbus, he was:
   a. A stuntman
   b. A ditch digger
   c. A Fuller Brush salesman
   d. All of the above
   e. None of the above

True or False

A. There was once a Playboy Club in Columbus

B. Walgreens and Gray's both had drugstores in downtown Columbus

C. Nancy Wilson and Rusty Bryant performed at Lou Wilson's Club Caroline

D. The Top, Dan's Drive-in and Rubino's were all founded in 1954.

E. The TAT Restaurant was named after an airline company.

F. George was the short order cook at the Feed Bag.

G. Bill Sapp and Lee Henry were not Polynesian.

H. Fat Cecilia Rosenthal ran the floral shop at Moby's

I. The theme song of The Early Worm was "Song of India".

The Answers:

1) C - Jane Rumberger

2) B - J.H. Pumphrey

3) A - University Club

4) C - Doersam's

5) C - Fort Hayes

6) A - Rogers and Company

7) B - Columbus Cadillac

8) C - The Fashion

9) A - Heaton's

10) F - Diehl Office Supply

11) All of them

12) C – Moby's

13) B – Ruby Cohen

14) D – All of the above

True or False - All of the answers are true.

RADIO AND TV PERSONALITIES

When we were kids we listened to the radio for the simple reason that there were no televisions. Jack Benny, Charlie McCarthy, Red Skelton, Bob Hope, Johnny Dollar, Boston Blackie, Inner Sanctum, The Shadow and Gang Busters, among others, became our fantasy world. Also, on numerous occasions, we would sit around the radio and listen to F.D.R. give us encouragement concerning the war efforts during World War II.

During the war years (1941-1945) Chet Long, sponsored by the gas company, gave us the news and Irwin Johnson, known as "the early worm" played records. Soon after the war a new breed of radio and TV personalities entered the scene.... Some of the notables.

> Marty DeVictor -- WBNS Radio
> Spook Beckman -- WTVN Radio
> Fritz the Nite Owl -- WBNS TV
> Dave Logan -- WTVN Radio
> Gene Fullen -- WTVN Radio
> Bob Connors -- WTVN Radio
> Rod Serling -- WBNS TV
> Jonathan Winters -- WBNS TV
> Flippo the Clown -- WBNS TV
> Jimmy Crum -- WCMH TV
> Perry Frey -- WTVN Radio Manager
> Hugh DeMoss -- WBNS TV
> Lucille Gasaway -- "Luci's Toy Shop" on WBNS TV

Today it is shock radio, rock music and talk radio. Our link to the past is the "Morning Monarch" - Bob Connors at WTVN Radio. He is as good as it gets!

The Huntington National Bank Building

The former Madison's Store at 72 North High Street.

The Columbus Dispatch headquarters.

American Electric Power Headquarters

The Arbor Inn

The Atlas Building

Thomas L. Carey, Clothing Store

The Board of Trade Building

Bott Brothers Billiards (aka The Clock Restaurant)

The Busy Bee Restaurant

Charbert's Drive-in

The Clarmont Restaurant

Forester's Restaurant

The original Wendy's Restaurant

State Automobile Mutual Insurance

Ohio State Life Insurance Company

The Ohio State Journal

The Lindenhoff Restaurant (aka Lindey's)

MEMORIES

According to……

I interviewed the following people about their experiences downtown and the surrounding area. In each case I asked basically the same question, "What do you remember about Columbus and the community of yesteryear?" In the pages that follow you will find the responses to that question and various other memories of Columbus. I thank each of them for sitting down with me so that they could revisit the golden years of Columbus. Their input was invaluable.

If you doubt any of their recollections, please call them, not me!!!

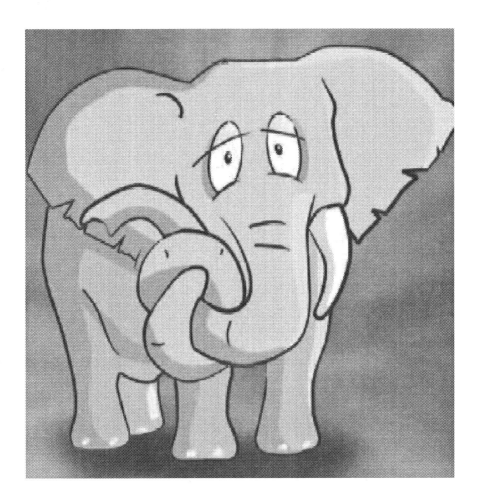

Martin Adler

Marty and his family immigrated to the United States in 1938 when he was 10 years old. He attended the Ohio Avenue School, Roosevelt Junior High School and four years later graduated from East High School. He was a star football and baseball player.

During the Second World War, Marty, as a teenager, had a great job as a roller skating instructor at Rollerland, which was located at the corner of 18th and Mound. At OSU Marty's roommates were Vic Janowicz and Skippy Doyle.

During his college years, Marty frequented jazz clubs and one night he witnessed the best saxophone player he had ever heard, Rusty Bryant. His signature song was "Night Train". As a favor to his future father-in-law, Lou Wilson, who owned Club Caroline, Marty introduced Lou to Rusty. Rusty became a legend at Club Caroline on Marion Road for many years. His band also featured a young and talented sixteen year old female singer by the name of Nancy Wilson. Nancy went on to achieve national fame and Rusty continued to play "Night Train".

In 1948 Marty entered the service and was discharged in 1952. Upon returning he worked at Star-Nelson Furniture store at Main and Fourth Streets. A few years later he and Bobby Schiff created a partnership in the furniture business on Hamilton Road. Since 1978, Marty has owned and operated Bexley Travel Agency, a full-service travel agency.

What Marty recalls most about Columbus during the 40's, 50's and 60's are such haunts as the Dugout, Jan Van's and the Far East. He also remembers Mogol's menswear and the Boston Store. Marty reminded me that Moby's had a grocery department in the middle of its first floor. Even Lazarus couldn't match that!

Arline and Jerry Altman

Jerry Altman was born in 1933. His parents were Sam and Natalie. The family lived and worked in Athens, Ohio where they owned a department store. Jerry graduated from the Greenbriar Military School in 1950 and OSU in 1954. He became a psychiatrist in Columbus, Ohio in 1963. He has been a lifelong member of Temple Israel and has fond memories of downtown, where he has visited thousands of times for both work and pleasure.

Some of Jerry's favorite things downtown…

1. Lazarus - the men's clothing department
2. The Union - their shirt selection
3. Marzetti's - the minestrone soup
4. The Maramor - floating island
5. The Street Cars - a six cent ride
6. Kuenning's - milk-fed fried veal

Arline is from St. Louis, Missouri where her dad was a pharmaceutical manufacturer. Her grandfather's aunt founded the business in 1876, which would have been highly unusual for a woman in those days. She met Jerry through his twin sister, with whom she taught school in St. Louis. Jerry and Arline married in 1962 in St. Louis and immediately moved to Ohio.

Arline remembers……

1. The Maramor - food and CANDY
2. Montaldo's - the finest clothes
3. The Union - beautiful displays
4. Kahn's Jewelry Store - fine diamonds
5. Marzetti's - a lobster dish with mashed potatoes on the edges

Jerry's friends call him the "crazy doctor" - get it? He is a shrink. Arline has spent her professional career as a private college placement counselor. She has also been an active participant of the Temple Israel community.

They are a wonderful, caring couple who have made Columbus, Ohio a better place to live.

KUENNING'S SUBURBAN RESTAURANT
3015 East Main Street, U. S. Highway 40 East, Columbus, Ohio

Mike Callif

The Central Market -- Back in the 1890's when parking meters were hitching posts that didn't require nickels and dimes for the privilege of their use. The Central Market was the hub of downtown commerce. Seventy years later the marketplace at Fourth and Rich Streets was still a thriving center of commerce although the heart of the city had moved to Broad and High Streets.

In the early 1960's, the 115 year old market had outlived its usefulness and the city of Columbus wanted to tear it down to make way for new development. However, history buffs and shopkeepers who had stores in the old facility fought the move in the courts and the polls. The battle raged for nearly six years before the block-long building was finally razed. The Greyhound bus station and the IBM office building now stand on the site of the former marketplace.

In 1949 some of the produce merchants working in this building were:

- Caito Brothers
- Columbus Fruit and Vegetable Company
- William Fean and Company
- Edward Hertlein & Company
- Kauffman and Goldslager
- Philip's Office Brothers
- Roth's Market
- Sugar Produce
- Wolman & Gelin
- William Callif and Sons

Around 1900, Mike's grandfather, William, founded William Callif and Sons which provided fruits and vegetables for restaurants. Mr. Callif's sons, Paul and Herbie, took over the business in 1958. In 1976 Mike and his brother Bill inherited the business when Paul, their father, passed away.

In 1984 Mike sold the business to Continental Coffee Company but bought it back in 1987. He still runs it today. The Callif produce business has been around continuously in Columbus for 109 years.

Mike has vivid memories of starting work at 2:00 am and working to mid-afternoon. He still does it today. In those early days the market was teeming with people. The merchants were a group of Catholics, Jews and Italians who were constantly arguing, but also got along, pushing their fruits and vegetables. Simply put, the market was orderly chaos.

Mike's favorite haunts were the Eastmoor and Town House drive-ins plus the Far East and the Feed Bag. Of course, Kuenning's, Presutti's, The Jai Lai, Kahiki, Reeb's and the Top were his favorite night time eating establishments. If you wanted to know which restaurants were "making it" or which new restaurants were going to open soon, just see Mike! You still can today.

Presutti's Villa Restaurant

Steve Cartwright

Steve's father Todd came to Columbus in 1921. He moved here from Maine where he was in the shoe business. His mother's name was Josephine (Jo). Mr. Cartwright sold bonds for the Ohio National Bank before moving over to Blair and Company. He eventually joined Sweney in 1946 to form Sweney-Cartwright located at 17 South High Street, the original Huntington Bank building. As of 2009, they have been tenants for 63 years.

Steve joined the firm in 1959. He is both a lifelong resident of Bexley and downtown. Steve has lived his entire life within a mile and a half of where he was born. That's stability!

Steve, fondly and with passion, remembers Mill's for it large breakfasts, featuring fried mush. I thought you could only get mush at the Waffle House. Wonders never cease! He loved Kuenning's and the stag grill at the Neil House. The Deshler featured the Hour Glass Bar and the Madrid Room. They served a fabulous Hollywood salad.

The brokerage firms of the 1940's, 1950's and 1960's were:

- Bache
- Vercoe
- John B. Joyce Company
- Merrill Lynch
- Paine Webber
- Smith Barney
- The Ohio Company
- Samuel & Engler
- Lorenz and Company

Steve reminded me that as teenagers in the 1950's we all wore Spalding's black and white saddle shoes and we purchased them from Smith and Lee on East Broad Street. Do you remember?

103

Today, Steve is alive, kicking and still working. His firm specializes in corporate and municipal bonds. In a recent visit to Steve's office, he commented to me that in 2009 there is not one place downtown to buy clothes, not even a handkerchief. In 1955 there were at least 1,000 establishments downtown, today there are literally none.

Is this progress or what?

The Neil House Hotel

Barbara Drugan

We all know that the greatest compliment you can give another person is to remember his or her name. In Barbara's case she gives compliments to "everyone" she greets because she never forgets a name. Not only your name, but also every member of your family. How does she do it?

While she is a legend in name recognition, her real talent was that of the world's best kindergarten teacher at Cassingham Elementary. Her name is synonymous with Bexley education.

Her parents were Ed and Gertrude Drugan. Mr. Drugan and Al Harmon's father were partners in a property and casualty insurance agency during the 1930's called Archer, Meek, Harmon and Drugan.

Barbara graduated from Saint Mary of the Springs in 1943 and the School of Education at OSU in 1947. She lived in Eastmoor and rode her bike to Montrose Elementary in 1946 to do her student teaching. At that time, Montrose had the only kindergarten program in the city of Bexley. Some of her early students were John B. McCoy, Steve Tuckerman, Steve DeVol and Bill Hayes.

In 1950, Maryland Avenue School was built and during that same year Cassingham Elementary opened its own kindergarten class. Barbara was a fixture at Cassingham from 1950 until 1979, the year she retired.

Of course, she remembered every student from every class. I asked her to mention a few and I couldn't write them fast enough. She rattled off Bruce Friedman, Dr. Bill Salt. Clark Knowles, Silvia Dozier, Marcia Ziskind, Debbie Kayne, Jack Roth, Diane Mathless, Danny Dick, Holly Davidson, Eddie Weston, Bobby Schwartz, Mark Smilak, Nancy Glick, Diane Garek, Chuck Schenk and Jeffrey Grossman.

Barbara recalls with fond memories that every Thursday her mother and Allen Gundersheimer's mother had lunch together. They never missed that date. The Drugans are Catholic and the Gundersheimers are Jewish. It was a family mandate of her parents that everyone must get along with each other. Barbara certainly does that well. Barbara's new best friend is only a handshake away.

She loved going to lunch at Lazarus and visiting the Maramor for their fabulous and famous dessert - Floating Island.

If you want to know "anything" about the history of Bexley or the school system, stop by Wing's on any Sunday evening around six. She and Bill Emig will fill you in on any missing links. Truly Miss Barbara is a legend in her own time.

This is Miss Barbara's afternoon kindergarten class from 1948.
Can you name these people?
Can you pick out John B. McCoy* in this photo?

*Answer: 2nd row, 1st student on the left

Mark Feinknopf

Mark's maternal great, great, grandfather was the second Rabbi of Temple Israel here in Columbus. Mark's father graduated from Walnut Hills in Cincinnati and in 1913 graduated as an architect from OSU. He served in World War I and in 1918 became a partner with Leo Yassenoff in a firm called F & Y Construction Company. The partnership lasted ten years until Mr. Feinknopf decided to start his own private architecture and construction company. In 2009, the firm has survived successfully for 81 years. Mark's father died in 1984

Mark graduated from the Columbus Academy in 1954, Yale in 1958, followed by the Harvard School of Design. Mark graduated number one in his class at Harvard.

Mark joined the firm in the early sixties and helped run it successfully until he sold his interest to his partners in 1997.

When I spoke with Mark concerning downtown during the 40's, 50's and 60's he came to the same conclusions as others, that when the regional malls opened they drew all the shoppers away from downtown. When the shoppers leave, the restaurants close and everything else simply deteriorates.

The hope was that with the opening of the City Center shopping mall in 1989 housing would follow, but that didn't happen either. Mark also explained that around 1990, seven other downtown malls opened throughout the country and none have succeeded.

As a planner, Mark worked on many downtown projects throughout the country. I asked him, "Will downtown ever become viable like it once was?" His viewpoint is that:

1. You need housing first
2. Buildings and stadiums are not a continual draw for people
3. Lack of ability to move people around downtown is disastrous
4. People need to work and walk in the same area

However, Mark suggested that I need not despair. Back in the 1960's, Don Weaver, a columnist for the Columbus Dispatch told Mark to just look at Paris, France. Its downtown has dried up six or seven times but each time it rejuvenated itself as a brand new downtown. Perhaps with the new housing downtown, in time, it will happen in Columbus.

Mark currently lives in Atlanta, but visits regularly, keeping in touch with family and friends. I just wish he had the magic pill to resurrect the glory days of downtown. Until that happens, we at least have fond memories. I guess we should be thankful for what we had and hope it will return someday soon.

Capital Square of the 1950's

Barbara Ornstein Feurer

Barbara and her first husband, George, were married in New York City in 1953. They moved to Columbus in 1956. George was working on his Ph.D. at OSU and soon after secured a position at North American Rockwell on East Fifth Avenue.

In 1961 they moved to Bexley. During the 1960's and 70's, with two small children, they didn't spend too much time going to nightclubs or fancy restaurants. George eventually left Rockwell and joined R.G. Barry Corporation, founded by Florence and Aaron Zacks. Unfortunately George passed away in 1992.

As I have asked others about their entertainment, dining and clothing store memories Barbara related these remembrances.

1. Montaldo's – unequaled quality of their products and services
2. Kuenning's - the roast beef
3. Mill's – their fabulous soups
4. Lazarus - the Chintz Room
5. The Union - a class act store
6. Madison's - good values
7. Marzetti's - the seafood platter
8. The Clarmont - the banana cream pie
9. The Jai Lai - their vagabond stew
10. The Top - their steaks were the best
11. Meadowbrook - the peach pies
12. Ciro's - just like New York, almost

Barbara married Norman Feurer, a retired high school principal and assistant superintendent from Dayton, Ohio in 2007. They travel extensively (mostly cruising) and between her family and his they have many places to keep them occupied fulltime.

As Barbara said to me recently, "it's more fun to relive the past and all the fun that we had than it is to rock in our rocking chairs today".

The Christopher Inn

Vic and Elaine Goodman

When it comes to food, Vic Goodman is a gourmand. He plans vacations based upon where and when he is going to eat. His parents were Willie and Min and his younger sister is Paula. Vic graduated from the Columbus Academy followed by Yale and then Harvard Law School. He practiced with Topper and Alloway for years before joining the Benesch law firm. He is a labor lawyer and lobbyist.

He still enjoys beginning his day at the breakfast table with his friends at the Clarmont. The boys he eats with each morning feel they have a pulse on what is happening or going to happen in Columbus. I assume that just like any other group of old guys they have it all figured out. Maybe yes, maybe no. When he thinks of days gone by he remembers Lazarus first and foremost including:

1. Taking violin lessons at Lazarus
2. The Front Street Level for cake balls
3. The Tea Room for the hidden sandwich
4. The toy department

He loved eating at Paoletti's for lunch, especially the spaghetti omelet and the fresh baked pies. He enjoyed coconut cream pie at the University Club as well. When Vic and Elaine's son Jeffrey became a Bar Mitzvah he held the luncheon at the University Club. Herman Leochler, the club manager, had never catered a Jewish affair. Vic's instructions were simple, lots of good food and easy on the liquor. Vic said that Jews are eaters, not drinkers.

Elaine was born in 1938 and was the daughter of Richard and Jean Goldstein. Her father, during World War II, worked at Curtis Wright building airplanes for the war. When Elaine was eight they moved to Bexley at 762 Vernon Road. She vividly remembers:

1. Lazarus had a victory window display
2. Seeing Elsie the Cow at Lazarus
3. Shopping at the Boston Store and Bradford Hush
4. Going to the Central Market on Saturdays with her parents
5. Shopping at the Union
6. Luckoff's and the dime stores being fun places to visit
7. Practically living at the Glass Bowl in Bexley

Vic and Elaine have each contributed much to the Columbus community over the years. Vic has served on many boards and committees and his most vocal outbursts have to do with liberal politics. How can he be a Republican labor lawyer? It simply doesn't make sense!

Elaine is a pretend (her word) chef and has devoted countless years to enhancing the culinary tastes of Columbusites. Her many years of cooking classes at Lazarus/Macy's are a testament to her devotion to fine dining.

With Vic, the eater, and Elaine, the chef, this is a marriage made in heaven and one that has lasted 52 years.

The Chintz Room at Lazarus

Lois Greenblott

Morris (Mo) and Rose Garek, Lois' parents, were both born in 1913. They both graduated from high school in 1931. Mo from East High School and Rose from Bexley High School. Morris's father was a tailor and Rose's father owned a lumber store in Johnstown, Ohio. They married in 1933 and in 1935 Lois was born. She had a brother, Bobby . Her little sister Diane is a Bexley resident.

After graduating from high school Mo started his business career with Montgomery Ward. A few years later he joined Lazarus and with good old fashioned hard work and a great head on his shoulders became Vice-Chairman of the store. Not a bad career for a high school graduate.

In 1949, Lois and her family moved to Bexley and in 1956 she married David Madison, the future mayor of Bexley. Since her father worked at Lazarus, she spent a great deal of time at the store. In high school Lois had the largest collection of Pringle cashmere sweaters in the city. Her female classmates envied her greatly. I think her dad might have spoiled her just a bit??!

Lois has many fond memories of downtown during our golden era. These include:

- You could safely take the bus downtown and make it home without harm
- Marzetti's was the most fabulous eating experience in Columbus
- She loved the record department at Lazarus (The Best In Town)
- The Chintz and Colonial dining rooms at Lazarus were "to die for"
- She also adored the hidden sandwich on rye bread and the famous celery dressing
- Next door to Lazarus was Baker's shoes. Girls could have their prom shoes dyed to match their dresses. By the way, most proms were held at Valley Dale.
- She also recounted seeing Elsie the Cow and Lassie at Lazarus.

For entertainment in those days it was either downtown or Buckeye Lake at the amusement park or the Crystal or Pier Ballrooms. Lois also related on one

113

occasion that a group of her girlfriends went to the Gaiety Burlesque on South High. Whatever they learned they never showed us!

She also remembers the original airport on East Fifth Avenue near Hamilton Road as well as the dog cemetery. I wonder what was going on at the dog cemetery, especially in a car at night. Whatever happened at the dog cemetery stayed at the dog cemetery.

Allen Gundersheimer

Allen Gundersheimer's family arrived in Columbus from Germany in 1840. The population of Columbus at that time was 5,000. Allen's grandfather was S.M. Levy who founded The Union department store in 1894.

Allen's father started the Fashion in 1924 and located it directly across the street from Lazarus. Next door to the Fashion was a second department store called Morehouse-Martin's which was owned by Allied, a national department store conglomerate. In 1948 Morehouse-Martin's wanted to expand so they purchased The Fashion and the new name was Morehouse-Fashion. Please remember this as there will be a quiz later.

Allen Gundersheimer Sr. did not graduate from high school but through hard work became a bookkeeper for a bank. Years later he and a Mr. Reiser became partners in founding The Fashion.

Allen Jr. graduated from Bexley High School in 1940 and in 1942 during his sophomore year at OSU enlisted in the Navy. He was discharged from the service in 1945 and joined The Fashion. He married Muriel in 1947 and in 1950 transferred to The Union until his retirement in 1980.

Allen acknowledges the fact that Lazarus set the rules when it came to store hours. When Lazarus decided to be open on Monday evenings it forced every other department store downtown to follow suit. The other stores hated having to adjust their workforce to comply with what Lazarus was doing.

Also Allen tells me that during the 40's and 50's each store had its own charge accounts. There were no Visa, Amex, or Mastercards. Lazarus had more charge accounts per population than any store in the United States.

Allen loved downtown and especially:

o   Marzetti's for its fabulous spaghetti and it's risotto
o   Mill's Cafeteria and Restaurant
o   The Maramor
o   The QCB Restaurant, a breakfast joint on North High Street

In Bexley, he recalled:

- o   The Far East
- o   The Glass Bowl
- o   Merkle's Drive-In

Allen told me something that I had not known. The Gundersheimers, the Lazaruses, and the Nussbaums were the first Jewish settlers in Columbus, around 1840. In fact, all three families were instrumental in founding Temple Israel in 1846, which is the oldest Jewish religious organization in Central Ohio. Without Lazarus, The Fashion and The Union, downtown Columbus would have been very ordinary.

In 1968 The Fashion closed its doors forever. What a fabulous business establishment.

The Riviera Restaurant

Alfred W. Harmon
(1925 – 2009)

At 5' 7" Al Harmon was a giant of a man. I cannot name one person who ever met Al who did not immediately like him. As owner and TV spokesman for the Original Mattress Factory he became somewhat of a celebrity in town. People watching the commercials admired Al as a trusting and down to earth person. Sales climbed dramatically.

Al's father came to Columbus in 1894 and established an insurance agency called Meeks, Drugan and Harmon. They specialized in property and casualty coverage for downtown retail stores like Lazarus, The Union, Madison's and The Fashion. When Alfred Harmon Sr. died in 1938 Al's mother, Amy, continued running the agency for the next three years before selling to her brother Robert Weiler Sr.

In 1940, Amy married Simon Lazarus and they moved to 172 South Columbia Avenue in Bexley. Al graduated from The Columbus Academy in 1944 and instead of entering college he worked at The Citizen-Journal newspaper in the advertising department. This first real job launched his career as a great marketer. In addition to his advertising activities at the newspaper he was asked to write a Sunday article on "Golf," a subject he knew absolutely nothing about. He had never played golf nor had he even been to a golf tournament. However, his writing skills surpassed his knowledge of golf and according to Al he was a success. Every Saturday night around 11:00pm he would show up at the Dell restaurant on Parsons Avenue to secure an early Sunday edition of the newspaper. His article had his picture and by-line.

A few months passed and guess what happened…..he got fired! His boss said he was a lousy speller and should go to college and get a degree. He was promised a job upon graduation. In the next six months he attended OSU and then decided he wanted to go away to college. He entered Oberlin College, went out for the football team and was the fifth string quarterback and a defensive end. The result of his athletic endeavors was a broken leg.

Somewhere along the way he neglected to tell his mother about his football career and of course she put an end to such activities. He graduated from

117

Oberlin in 1948 with a major in history. At a job fair at Lazarus he was hired as a stockman, but quickly was promoted to the assistant buyer in charge of mattresses. The mattress business was in his blood the remainder of his life.

In 1953 Al was earning $6,500 annually when Sealy Mattress Company offered $10,000 plus a car. Al and his wife Sue could not turn down this fabulous offer. He eventually became V.P. and Sales Manager for Sealy until 1977 when he resigned.

In the middle and late 1970's, Al was president of the Bexley School Board and Winding Hollow Country Club. Also during this time he was a fifty percent owner of Ruth Wilson Floor Coverings. In 1981 he sold his interest in the company and obtained real estate and stock brokerage licenses (he hated both). In 2000, he became a distributor for automated external defibrillators (A.E.D.). What a long and distinguished career.

Al remembered, as a youth, taking the bus downtown so that he could go to Lazarus to buy a milkshake. As a Bexley resident he fondly recalled the Glass Bowl, Wentz Drug Store, the Far East and Van's Drive-in.

Al's death in January 2009 was a devastating loss to family, friends and the general community. I valued Al's friendship dearly. It was a great personal loss for me! I have never known anyone who had the ability to always be positive when things were not always positive. Whenever I needed advice and counsel on business matters he was only a phone call away. When it came to golf he was always proud of the fact that he NEVER was a good golfer so that shooting 100 was okay with him. For twenty-five years I toiled with him on the golf links and I enjoyed every minute of being with him.

Al Harmon was a giver, not a taker. He was a listener, not a talker. He was everyone's friend. We were fortunate to have known him. I know I was!

Bill Harrison

I have known Bill since he entered the life insurance business some 44 years ago. He has served the insurance industry with distinction. In fact, he recently completed his term as President of the Columbus Chapter of the National Association of Insurance and Financial Advisors (NAIFA-Columbus). What I didn't know was the fact that back in 1961 he was the first maitre' d of the Kahiki. Wonders never cease.

Bill was in the military (on our side) for 10 years during the 1950's. His very first job upon arriving in Columbus in 1960 was working for Barry Kessler, a public accountant. He earned $1.25 per hour. Bill tells the story that Bill Sapp and Lee Henry of the Kahiki interviewed 125 individuals for the maitre' d position. Because of his sparkling personality and good looks he landed the job. He remembers being paid $125 per week. Bill Harrison will always be linked to both the Kahiki and the Jai Lai.

The Kahiki Years - As we know, the owners of the Kahiki were Bill Sapp and Lee Henry. They created a great and lasting partnership. Bill Sapp was the "in-house" person and Lee Henry was the "financial" person. In further discussions with Bill Harrison, he related some facts about the Kahiki that were quite interesting to me and hopefully to you as well...

- The average wait for a table in the first two years of business was 2 hours.
- They employed Sandro Conti, a true mixologist to create each and every drink.
- All the drinks were potent - each filled with lots of rum.
- Conti named each drink. For example, Harrison complained to Conti that there was no drink named after him (Bill) so the next day a brand new drink was created called "The Suffering Bastard". Harrison is so proud of this concoction. It had four and one half ounces of 100 proof rum and it knocked you on your butt.
- Henry and Sapp entertained dignitaries in their private offices. Dining tables were set and no two hour waits. As Bill Harrison always said, "It's great to be a big shot. The lines are shorter!"

- After dinner they offered jasmine scented warm towels to clean your hands.
- One evening a female customer stole a tiki lamp from the table and Bill, being the faithful employee and maitre' d saw what had just happened. He suggested to the guest that if she was interested in buying a lamp that they were for sale in the gift shop. She denied having the lamp and he responded by saying that there was kerosene dripping from her mink coat onto the floor. Her response was simple and direct,"Ooops". Isn't it amazing what we remember happening some 48 years ago.

The Jai Lai Years - In 1963 Bill was approached by the Jai Lai to become the daytime manager. They knew of his experience at the Kahiki. By simply doubling his pay it was easy for Bill to leave and join the Jai Lai family.

The unique feature of both the Kahiki and the Jai Lai was that every morsel of food served was homemade at the location. The prime rib and the vagabond stew at the Jai Lai were legendary food items. The place was always crowded and the atmosphere upbeat. The Jai Lai had a certain rhythm and atmosphere that made dining there extra special.

If you were lucky enough you may have seen Woody Hayes sitting at his table during the off-season discussing football and community affairs. Lee Corso, former Indiana coach tells the story that he would meet with Woody at the Jai Lai to find out which players Woody was "not" going to recruit. Lee then tried to recruit them to Indiana. Apparently it didn't work well as Corso's record at Indiana was dismal at best. Oh, by the way, Woody did not drink alcohol at the Jai Lai.

When I look back at the career of Bill Harrison I see a person who was in the Army (special forces), worked at the Kahiki and Jai Lai and today runs a highly successful full-service insurance agency. What a well rounded person.

Tad Jeffrey

Tad Jeffrey grew up in Sessions Village, graduating from the Columbus Academy in 1947 and Williams College in 1951, the same year he married Nancy Kittredge. By the way, Sessions Village is located on property that was previously F.C. Sessions' summer home. Tad received his MBA degree from Harvard in 1953.

Upon graduation from Harvard he entered the Navy and finally arrived back in Columbus in 1956. He joined the Jeffrey Company and in 1962 served as controller. Tad was president from 1968 to 1973. On May 3, 1974 the company was sold to Dresser Industries. Since 1974 Tad's responsibilities have been to manage the proceeds from the sale.

When I questioned Tad concerning his childhood memories of Columbus, he related some interesting tales:

- He fondly remembers Red Bird Stadium and the wonderful times he enjoyed watching those games.
- Taking the Oak Street bus downtown to roam the various business establishments.
- On many occasions he "went with" Jimmy Kobacker to Temple Israel where Rabbi Gup taught religious school. Tad admits that today his Hebrew is a little rusty.
- Walking to Wentz's drugstore soda fountain to savor a freshly mixed cherry Coke.
- Hanging out at the Glass Bowl
- Eating a sack of White Castles located next to Bexley City Hall
- Having a filet of sole dinner (with extra tartar sauce) at the Far East for a cost of seventy-five cents.

Tad's great grandfather founded the Jeffrey Companies, and it subsequently became an icon of a company, not only in Columbus, Ohio, but also all over the world.

121

A little more information about the beginnings of the Jeffrey Companies. Joseph A. Jeffrey, born on January 17, 1836, was the founder of the Jeffrey Manufacturing Company. He graduated high school from St. Mary's in Auglaize county. Mr. Jeffrey worked as a clerk in a general store before coming to Columbus in 1858. He gained employment at a bank and rose to the level of cashier, a very senior position in banking at that time. Soon after he left Columbus for Cincinnati and ventured into the wholesale and retail carpet and furniture business.

In 1869 he sold that business and returned to Columbus. During the same year he allied himself back in the banking business. The name of the bank was Sessions, and it subsequently became Bank One. He was the cashier until 1883 when he disposed of his interest to Mr. F.C. Sessions and entered full-time upon a manufacturing career.

He did this by acquiring a controlling interest in the Lechner Mining Machine Company, a concern struggling for existence. This was a bold step as it involved the development of an unproven invention consisting of a machine for cutting coal in mines, an innovation in the mining of coal.

The enterprise incorporated in 1877 with a capital stock of $50,000. Mr. Sessions, his former boss, was the first president. Mr. Jeffrey subsequently succeeded Sessions as president.

The scope of its operations was broadened in the successive stages of its history until Jeffrey Products became a byword in the coal trade of the U.S. and in foreign countries. The plant was the pride of Columbus manufacturing and commercial interests.

Tad served as its last president some 91 years later. His contributions, along with his wife Nancy, to both the business community and the general community have been enormous. Because of their love and caring, Columbus has been a better place to live.

Nye Larrimer

Nye's father, Richard, was one of the most colorful individuals to ever grace downtown Columbus. Nye's mother, Catherine, took charge of raising seven children, Nye, John, Terry (Deceased), Neil, Louise, Ellen and Margaret.

Mr. Larrimer was from Washington Courthouse and began his law career in the mid 1920's in downtown Columbus. He practiced general law until one day he received a call from John L. Lewis of the United Mine Workers of America asking if he would act as counsel representing the coal workers in a lawsuit. At that time in our history the coal mine owners had absolutely 100% control and power over the workers.

To everyone's surprise, R.N. Larrimer won the case and from that day spent his entire career on worker compensation issues representing the workers. His partner during those days was Clarence L. Corkwell. Their offices were on the fifth floor (facing south) at 44 East Broad Street. In fact, Corkwell placed a small sign in his window, plainly seen on Broad Street, stating that Corkwell was an attorney. Apparently the bar association had a fit and stated that "no self respecting lawyer would advertise". Nothing came of the complaint and the sign remained. The firm remained on Broad Street until they moved into the Larrimer Building on North High Street, just north of the Clock Restaurant.

For years the firm was managed by Gavin Larrimer, Nye's cousin and Nye's brother Terry. Today, Nye and Sara's son Kevin manages the firm. Since the 1920's the Larrimer law firm has been an institution - not a bad track record.

Nye's favorite restaurant was Marzetti's. His number two choice was Lutece in New York City. Every Sunday evening at 6:00pm, from 1945 on, the entire Larrimer clan dined at Marzetti's. In fact, since the bar was closed on Sundays, Carl Schaufele agreed to set a special table for the Larrimers in the middle of the bar.

If everyone behaved properly, Mr. & Mrs. Larrimer would take the family to a double-feature either at the Broad, Palace, Ohio or Grand Theaters. However, in 1971 Marzetti's closed and the era of fine dining in downtown Columbus was coming to an end. In fact, the closing of Marzetti's signaled the official notice - Sorry, Downtown Columbus Is Closed.

Looking back I asked what dishes made Marzetti's so special. Nye had this list for us:

- Seafood special (scallops, crab, sole, center of spaghetti)
- Filet of sole with tarter sauce
- Spaghetti
- French fries
- Minestrone soup
- Cole slaw
- Salad with French dressing
- Steaks
- Best martinis in Columbus
- Thousand Island dressing (always fresh)

Nye graduated from the Columbus Academy in 1954 (best class in the history of the school), Princeton in 1958 followed by medical school at OSU. In private practice with the Central Ohio Medical Group, Nye is a Board Certified Oncologist and internist. Today, Nye is retired and spends his time with his family and friends. He is a bona fide expert on OSU football, politics, fine dining and the theater. He will share his knowledge, just give him a call. You can count on him for his sage advice.

Marzetti's Restaurant circa 1951

Robert Lazarus Jr.

In 1851, Simon Lazarus opened the Lazarus store. His original store was a blockbusting 20 by 40 feet of space. He was the sole owner until 1872. In addition to owning and operating the store he became (without pay) the first Rabbi of Temple Israel. Simon had two sons, Fred and Ralph who worked in the store before and after school. Each morning Ralph went down to the Scioto River with a bucket to get water for mopping out the store before school.

Due to business growth, during and following the Civil War, salesmen were added and by 1868 Lazarus had seven salesmen. In the 1880's, visiting a general store to purchase men's clothing became increasingly popular. Realizing this, Simon invested $3,000 in stock and fixtures for a men's department within his store.

After the Civil War, the men's clothing department exploded with sales. In the late 1860's there were 200 menswear shops in Columbus, yes 200. Lazarus had two things going for longevity, the beginning of an adjustment policy; "It fits or you don't pay" and a set-price policy. Retailers of the period usually didn't mark the price on goods; rather they dickered over the price. Lazarus was one of the early converts to clearly marked prices on its goods. Customer service was the watchword of the store.

In 1877, Fred and Ralph became sole owners and partners; they changed the name of the store to F & R Lazarus. Both men did all of the buying, bookkeeping and some of the selling. Personnel were added gradually and by 1881 the store had 22 clerks. On August 9, 1909 a new six-story store opened on the northwest corner of Town and High Street. The original location had been at the southwest corner of Town and High. The population of Columbus at that time was 125,560.

In 1934, Lazarus added air conditioning. The store became a safe haven from the heat during those hot and sticky summer months. In 1946, the annex opened for the display and sale of house wares and home appliances.

During the 1950's, the store added four new restaurants: The Chintz Room, Buckeye Room, Copper Kettle and The Highlander Grill. Also during the late

1950's the first "air curtain" door in Central Ohio replaced the revolving doors at the High Street entrance. Interest in the new entrance was so great that more than one million leaflets explaining its operation were picked up by customers in the next few years. In 1950, Lazarus offered self-improvement courses for tweens and twixteens. For example, young girls learned how to walk on a style-show runway.

The Secret Gift Shop, a Lazarus invention, was introduced in 1957 and widely copied by stores all over the country. Young children could shop alone, no adults allowed except for staff helpers. They would pick out Christmas gifts for family and friends and then put the gifts into suitcase boxes they could open and close as often as they liked.

In the 1960's Robert Lazarus Sr. was Chairman and then became Chairman Emeritus. Charles Y. Lazarus was President until 1969 and then became Chairman. Robert Lazarus Jr. and Morris Garek were Executive Vice-Presidents. Blaine Evert was an Executive Vice-President from 1966 to 1969 and then President from 1969 to 1970.

The expansion of the Lazarus name began in 1962 with its first branch at Westland. Northland followed in 1964, Eastland in 1967, and Richland (near Mansfield) in 1969. These four branches encompassed some 900,000 square feet of floor space.

In 1970, Kingsdale opened and in 1971, the Home Store East at Eastland was created. In 1971, the Lima Mall store became operational and in 1973 the Capri Store in Town and Country Shopping Center on the east side of Columbus. During 1978 there were 1122 members of the 20-year club who had two decades or more of employment with Lazarus.

It's 2009 and F & R Lazarus and Company has gone missing. The journey began in 1851 with Simon Lazarus and today only Robert Lazarus Jr. remains. I call him the last Lazarus executive. Bob graduated from the Columbus Academy in 1945, joined the Navy and in 1950, graduated from Yale. He and Mary married in 1953 when he joined the store full-time. They have four children and six grandchildren. Bob started his career at Lazarus working during the Christmas season while in high school. He has fond remembrances of famous Bexley haunts such as:

- The chocolate sodas at Wentz Drug Store
- Chinese food at the Far East
- The Glass Bowl
- Frecker's for great hamburgers

126

He recounted how exciting it was to attend OSU football games as a youngster. Much has changed in Columbus but the thrill of OSU football will remain with us forever.

I want to thank Bob for taking the time to sit with me and tell me the Lazarus story. I have known Bob for many years, and his involvement in the community is legendary. Bob has chaired and championed many community causes from the United Way to the arts. Bob and Mary continue to be passionate community leaders. The name Lazarus is synonymous with Columbus, especially downtown shopping and community caring.

Sources: Robert Lazarus Jr.

                    <u>Lazarus Timetables</u>, a book published by the Lazarus Company

Don Levy

In 1890, S.M. Levy was passing through Columbus where he stopped by to see his old friend Governor William McKinley. The governor convinced S.M. to open a family clothing store downtown and in 1894 the Union was born. The friendship between S.M. and McKinley was so strong that at Mc Kinley's death Mr. Levy raised enough money to erect a statue of McKinley which faced the Neil House Hotel, where, as governor, he and his wife lived. The statute still stands in its original location today.

S.M. and his wife Hattie had six children. A daughter of S.M. was Fran Levy who married Allen Gundersheimer. They opened a store called The Fashion. More about that later.

The establishment that S.M. built at the corner of Long and High Streets was strictly a men's clothing store. Unfortunately, the store burned down not long after it was erected. In 1904 it was rebuilt. The store was called The Union in recognition of reuniting the country as a result of the end of the Civil War. After the store was rebuilt a women's clothing department was added. The building still exists today.

The Union was the first store to open a branch store at Lane Avenue in 1947. In the 1960's, with the environment changing, they decided to move across from Lazarus, the former location of the Fashion. Now they had plenty of floor space to really expand and become even more popular.

In the next generation the stores were run by Herbert and Robert K. Levy Sr. Bob Sr. was both a dynamic businessman and a civic leader. He became well-known as the "second mayor" of Columbus. The Levy family, from S.M. to Don and Bob Jr. set a high standard for what a beautiful and outstanding clothing store should look like.

The motto of The Union….

Home of Quality

Don, Herbert's son, graduated from the Columbus Academy in 1946 and met his wife Reva at the University of Iowa. They were married in 1950. They have four children and eight grandchildren. The eternally young and vivacious Don and Reva have escaped the beautiful year-round weather of Columbus, Ohio for Palm Desert, California. He always was a smart fellow.

Source: Don Levy
                    Ohio Jewish Chronicle Special Report

Tom Lynch

Tom Lynch, from Clyde, Ohio, graduated from Ohio University in 1961 with a B.S. in Education. From 1961 through 1968 Tom worked for Marvin Frank who owned the University Shop in Athens, Ohio. In 1968 Tom moved to their home office in Columbus and remained with Marvin until 1972. During this period he met Jerry Woodhouse who was the manager of their Miami University store in Oxford, Ohio.

In 1972, Tom and Jerry, against all advice, decided that there were enough lawyers, insurance, real estate people and politicians who still wore button-down shirts and blue blazers to open a store catering to the conservative look. The store was conveniently located on East Broad near Fourth Street. It was sandwiched between the Columbus and Athletic Clubs whose members alone provide at least 50% of its trade. Located next door to Woodhouse-Lynch was a men's shoe store, Barrie Ltd and Sabback's Children's Clothing.

In 1972, the competitors were Larry Rupp, Tom Carey, Harry Rook, Walker's, Dunhill's, Mogol's, Richmond's, The Union, Lazarus and Justin Thyme. It wasn't long before they either closed or drifted to the suburbs. Soon after opening their store, Jerry Woodhouse opted to leave the clothing business.

In 1972, downtown Columbus was either slowly dying or was already dead. In that same year, when Marzetti's restaurant called it quits after 76 years in business. Everyone seemed to understand that downtown was the place "not to be"!

Tom was the only merchant who bucked the flight to the suburbs. However, he did open branches in Worthington Square and Lane Avenue malls but in a few years he abandoned that effort. His life and business was downtown.

The burning question must be - how could Tom build this fabulous business in the world's worst business environment? I believe his secret was quite simple - build it and they will come. Tom Lynch was able to orchestrate great experiences with his customers. When you stopped by to chat with Tom you always:

- Were greeted with a sincere smile

- Heard some silly joke or story
- Received great service
- Bought more than you bargained for
- Felt good about Tom and the items you bought

Sadly, on February 29, 2008, Tom and his son decided that enough was enough. They had one final sale - turned out the lights, the party was over. Plant another flower on the grave of downtown Columbus.

Tom Lynch and his friends. Can you tell which one is Tom?

David Madison

David's parents, Louis and Jean were married in Cleveland, Ohio and moved to Columbus in 1930. Louis opened Madison's, a women's specialty store, at 72 North High Street. David tells me that as a youngster, his father took him downtown every Sunday morning to check out their store. They also walked down to Lazarus to study the window displays, especially the women's department. David hated that journey, especially in the winter months. During the 1940's, Madison's opened branches in Akron, Mansfield and Lima.

Jim Jacobs married David's sister Joyce and in 1956 joined the business. Louis died in 1957 with Jean assuming the office of President. David and Jim were Vice-Presidents. In 1959, the store expanded to Kingsdale shopping center and closed the other three branches. In 1961, stores were opened in Town & Country, Northland, Eastland and Westland shopping centers. The downtown store's volume decreased as soon as the outlying shopping centers grew and prospered. The competition for Madison's was Montaldo's, Milgrim's, Jane Rumberger, The Union, Lazarus and The Fashion.

Everyone who ever set foot in Madison's felt welcome. Its customer service was equal to Lazarus and displayed its merchandise beautifully. However, like all downtown stores, the scene could no longer support retailing after the regional shopping center era began. Their heyday was the 40's, 50's and 60's. In 1991, the stores were sold.

Back in 1975, David left the store. He became Mayor of Bexley in 1976, which lasted for 32 years. He never looked back - he never enjoyed retailing. While downtown he loved Jack and Benny's, the Continental, Mill's, Kuenning's, Marzetti's and the Hayes restaurants.

As a young man growing up in Bexley, David remembers Buckeye Lake, especially the beautiful wooden speed boats, the amusement park and the dance halls. In Bexley he loved the Glass Bowl, the Far East, Eastmoor and Town House Drive-ins plus his favorite breakfast place, The Feed Bag. By the time David became mayor they had almost all disappeared!

Not only was David Madison a legendary mayor and dedicated public servant, but also a revered and beloved hamburger griller.

Nancy & Terry Meyer

Terry's parents, Paul and Bertha were married in 1931. Paul was a radiologist and graduated from OSU Medical School in 1935. Terry graduated from Bexley High School in 1953, completed his undergraduate work at OSU, and graduated from medical school in 1960. After internship, residency and military service he came back to Columbus in 1966 as a radiologist.

Terry remembers living with his grandparents during World War II because his father was in the service. He remembers Leonard's Drug Store at the corner of Livingston and Parsons for its great soda fountain. In high school he visited, on more than one occasion, the Eastmoor, Town House, Van's and Merkle's Drive-ins, plus the Glass Bowl and for night life the famous Club Carolyn. When he could afford to he even dined at The Top restaurant. His buddies at that time were Bob Roth, Chuck Nuestadt, Bob Weiler, Jack Myers, David Folkman, Eddie Russell and Bob Koltun.

Nancy is from Gastonia, North Carolina and arrived in Bexley in 1952 beginning her junior year in high school. You guessed it; the first person she met was Terry, who took her for a tour of the school. Love at first sight! I'm not sure, but it sure sounds good! At age 16 she remembers going to her first Bexley High School dance with Terry.

When I asked Nancy and Terry about there recollections and remembrances of Columbus in the 50's, 60's and 70's they rattled off the following:

1. Ciro's - great night club
2. Deshler Wallick Sky Room - a beautiful view
3. Clarmont - great steaks
4. Marzetti's - first class
5. Kuenning's - fabulous salad
6. Mill's - super pies
7. Howard Johnson's - BEST ice cream
8. Emil's - oh, those great corned beef sandwiches
9. Massey's - the best pizza in Columbus
10. Lazarus/Morehouse Fashion/The Union - the best department stores in Columbus

11. Charbert's - great drive-in
12. Jay Van's - world's best ribs

Terry and Nancy lived on Merkle Road for many years and today they spend half of their time in Naples, Florida. They have three wonderful children and nine super grandchildren. Terry is still trying to improve his golf game and Nancy is the hostess with the mostest.

Mill's Restaurant

Dick Oman

In my estimation Dick Oman and the Columbus Foundation will forever be linked to each other. In 1914, the first community foundation was established in Cleveland, Ohio. In 1943, Frederick Goff of Cleveland and Harrison Sayre of Columbus started the Columbus Foundation. In 1955 Dick was the attorney for the foundation and from 1969-1977 served as Executive Director.

Dick started his career at Ohio National Bank in 1951 in the real estate department. He later joined the Mort Isaac law firm and in 1975 moved over to Porter Stanley. In 1990 he joined the Vorys firm and still enjoys working in probate and tax matters.

I asked Dick where he kept all of the business of the foundation in 1955. His response was easy to understand - "The top drawer of my desk at the office." The foundation in 1955 had $500,000, today it is approaching one billion dollars.

I can remember inviting Dick to speak dozens of times to various insurance and financial planners concerning the Columbus Foundation. Dick was always able and willing to devote any amount of time it took to promote and encourage people to contribute to this essential charitable vehicle. Columbus should never forget his contributions to the community, and I'm sure they won't.

Since Dick was definitely a downtown person I specifically asked him his recollections about what he remembered about the culture of Columbus years ago. Of course he remembers Marzetti's with its minestrone soup and fried oysters. He also remembers that Carl Schaufele would only allow each patron only two martinis at lunch. I verified this fact with Steve Cartwright who tells me his dad, Todd told him the same tale.

Dick also has fond memories of the Maramor and the Chintz Room at Lazarus. Dick frequented the Fort Hayes Crystal Ballroom and in 1955 joined the Columbus Club. He purchased his clothes from Pumphrey's and Tom Carey. At the Deshler there were semi-annual trunk shows from Brooks Brothers. From those days to the present the only shirts he wears are from Brooks Brothers.

Dick feels that the two most prestigious office buildings downtown are 88 and 100 East Broad Street. He loved the Hartman Theater and even going to the Columbus Symphony at Central High School. A number of years ago the Ohio Theater was going to be torn down. At a meeting in his living room it was decided to raise money and retain this beautiful theater. As they say, the rest is history.

Without dedicated individuals like Dick Oman our community would suffer dramatically. In his case maybe one billion dollars worth of suffering.

Jim Petropolous

Jim attended OSU in 1948 and graduated in 1953. His great buddy and roommate was none other than Heisman Trophy winner Vic Janowicz! They both worked for John Galbreath as construction workers during their college years. After graduating, Jim went to work with Galbreath full time as a residential real estate agent. The company was housed on the seventh floor of the Buckeye Building, a building that he later managed for many years.

Jim's desire was to sell commercial real estate, not residential, but John Galbreath would not agree. In 1956 he left Galbreath to launch his own real estate ventures. Along with partner, John McConnell he purchased not only the Buckeye Building but also all of the stock of Buckeye Federal Savings and Loan in 1987. In 1989 they sold it to National City.

It was back in 1955 that Jim first met John McConnell and in the late 80's he became a board member of Worthington Industries. He was also named a vice-president -- in charge of their lake!

I asked Jim what made downtown really work in the 50's, 60's and 70's and who were the players. Here are his thoughts…

1. John Elam at Vory's
2. John W. Wolfe and his involvement with the Columbus Foundation
3. John Galbreath being the visionary that he was
4. Jack Havens as the chairman of Bank One
5. Sherwood Fawcett as the head of Battelle
6. Dean Jeffers leading Nationwide Insurance
7. Judge Metcalf of the probate court

Jim Petropolous has been one of the movers and shakers of Columbus for many, many years. As past president of The Battelle Foundation and The Columbus Foundation he was instrumental in making certain that charitable monies were being channeled back into the community properly.

He was, and still is, one of the most charismatic individuals I have ever known. We are all lucky he landed in Columbus, Ohio. By the way, don't play gin rummy with him -- YOU WILL LOSE.

Buckeye Federal Savings and Loan inside and out

Jerry Saunders

Jerry's father moved from Florida to Columbus in the 1930's for a job as a construction worker. His mother soon followed. The migration of Blacks from the south during the 1930's made their way from downtown Union Station or the bus station over to Mount Vernon Avenue, which was a strip of businesses no more than a mile in length. Everything you needed you could find on Mt. Vernon Avenue. You could go to the Dunbar Theater and watch vaudeville acts and in the 1940's and 1950's you could go to the Pythian Theater (now the King Arts Complex) or the Cameo Theater and watch all-black movies that Hollywood had sent out into the hinterlands.

Along with these memorable landmarks, the avenue was home to the popular Chesapeake Food Bar, Lee's Fashion Store, Tyler's Drugs and the Vernon Club. Toward the end of the 1950's many business owners moved East into Bexley selling stores and shops to blacks. For example, Tom Paige purchased the Club Jamaica, Marcellus Thurman bought The Vernon Club and George Berry, the Chesapeake Food Bar. Today, with urban renewal and the construction of I-670 all has changed. Gone are those fabulous establishments. At one time Carl Brown owned the largest black-owned grocery store in America.

In 1983, real estate expert William Potter convinced Bill Williams to open a restaurant/jazz club inside the Mount Vernon Plaza. Williams wanted a place that was nice and comfortable because he was upset that many evenings he would ride down the avenue with friends and there was no nice place to go like they had in the old days. When he thought of what he would name it he thought of his youth in the city, of the marathon games of marbles he and childhood friends used to play. In those days gangs were gentle, a fraternity of boys at play. Thus, he named his restaurant the Marble Gang.

Now the Marble Gang is no more; a clothing store has replaced it. So much for the avenue as we knew it.

Back to the family. Mr. Saunder's real mission was that of a minister. Their given name was Sanders, named after slave owners but changed to Saunders when they moved up north. Now it is their "family" name not their "given" name. Jerry has three sisters and one brother, Fred, who was a great basketball player for the Boston Celtics.

Jerry was born at OSU Hospital on April 23, 1953 at 10:25pm (Room 504). I guess some people are really good at remembering times and dates. Jerry graduated from Mohawk High School in 1971 as class president, number three in academic ranking, plus an all-star basketball player. He graduated from Oberlin college where he was captain of the basketball team his sophomore, junior and senior years. He played semi-pro ball for 18 months and coached the women's pro team, the Columbus Minks in 1985. Jerry worked at the Eastside YMCA from 1987 to 1997 and in 1998 married his lovely wife Gayle. Their son Jerry Jr. turned 5 in 2009.

I asked Jerry what restrictions (if any) his family had put on him during his youth. This is what he remembered:

- Don't travel to the South
- Bexley and Upper Arlington were off-limits
- Don't go downtown

He was told that Mt. Vernon Avenue and Long Street had all the stores that he needed. Stay close to home because it was safer. Jerry was just a plain solid honor student who went to church. Isn't that refreshing.

Since 1997, Jerry has devoted his entire energies to the community. He was with the ADAMH Board dealing with substance abuse and today he is the CEO of the Africentric Personal Development Shop, Inc. (APDS) which is an organization devoted to outpatient and treatment services.

It once again proves that with a strong education and strong religious background you can create whatever you want in life. Jerry Saunders is a prime example.

Source: The Columbus Post - February 22-28, 2001, "The Good Ol' Days"

Jay Schoedinger

The Schoedinger Funeral Home is the oldest continuing business in Columbus, Ohio. When the Schoedingers arrived in Columbus in the 1830's the population was approximately 3,000 individuals.

Phillip Schoedinger founded the funeral home in the early 1850's. He started as a carpenter in the furniture building trade. At that time most coffins were ordered from local carpenters. It was not unusual for a carpenter to add the lucrative business of undertaking to his business. In those days, embalming was not common. The undertaker's duties involved essentially providing the coffin, transporting the deceased to the cemetery, and arranging for the burial.

When Philipp died on May 28, 1880 his estate included four life insurance policies totaling $7,000 plus three pieces of downtown property and the undertaking business worth some $4,000. In those days, caskets cost $10.00. His son George, at age thirty, inherited the business.

Embalming became a standard procedure after the Civil War and the work of funeral directors expanded and progressed from a trade to a profession. In 1893 the code of conduct for funeral directors stated:

1. Don't talk too much: Your patrons don't want gas.
2. Don't get big-headed: There are other people on earth.
3. Don't wear squeaky shoes: It makes folks tired.
4. Don't be careless in dress: It shows bad breeding.
5. Don't swear: It is a sin against God.
6. Be a gentleman: Even rowdies respect such.
7. Be firm: Stand ever for right.
8. Be a student: If new methods are best, use them.

In 1912, the funeral home purchased the first motor hearse in Central Ohio. In 1916, George died and his half-brother Albert became principal director until his death in 1932.

The modern home of Schoedinger's Funeral Services is located at 229 East State Street. It was opened in 1919 and still today remains one of the most beautiful funeral facilities in the nation. The business kept growing and prospering because it provided a service with dignity at a reasonable price. The Schoedinger watch word, according to Jay, is "The customer is always right!" Old words, but true meaning.

It was in 1950 that they acquired and operated their first chapel outside downtown Columbus. In fact, all of their growth has been through acquisitions. Today, Schoedinger is providing the same quality of service as it did back in the 1800's. Is there a secret for its success? Maybe it is this.....

1. There are no absentee owners -- you work there!
2. No coupon clippers!

It's amazing what you can learn in six or seven generations.

Jay graduated from the Columbus Academy in 1958, attended OSU for two years and graduated from mortuary school in 1963. He is a fifth generation Schoedinger and served as president of the company for many years. Jay has always been a "downtowner". As a youngster he loved visiting Lazarus at Christmas time to view the fabulously decorated front windows and visit the toy shop on the sixth floor. Jay especially loved the Lionel train display and became a collector of Lionel trains.

He also remembers the fence that surrounded the state house and the newsstand on the southeast corner of Broad and High. His favorite restaurants were Marzetti's, Kuenning's and especially The Maramor where, as a kid, each youngster was given a toy box with candy inside.

The Schoedinger family is unique for their longevity in business. In the last 154 years their name has become synonymous with dignified funeral services. What a great family tradition to emulate.

Source: *"A History of the Schoedinger Family from Döorenbach,*
                Germany to Columbus, Ohio and Beyond"
                Jay Schoedinger

Jack Stephan

Herschel Stephan, Jack's father, was born in Newark, Ohio in 1897 and died in Columbus in 1997 at age 100. He graduated from Newark High School in 1914 and Ohio Wesleyan in 1919 as a chemistry major. In 1920 he married Dorothy Kramer, moved to Columbus, and entered the insurance business that very same year with the Travelers. Jack's older brother, William, graduated from the Columbus Academy in 1944, went on to medical school and today is a retired physician in Las Vegas.

Three generations of the Stephan family, Herschel, Jack and Jack's son Jay have been a downtown fixture in the insurance business for over 88 years. Herschel, a legend in the insurance industry, was president of the Columbus Life Underwriter's Association in 1935 and later founded COSI (Center of Science & Industry).

In 2004, Herschel was chosen to receive the Columbus Life Underwriter's coveted Lifetime Achievement Award. The award is given only to those insurance professionals who have distinguished themselves both in the insurance industry and the community at large.

In 1926, the Stephans lived in Bexley on North Ardmore before moving to South Cassingham Road in 1930. Herschel, as a civic minded individual, was a member of Bexley City Council and the school board. He was a very dedicated volunteer.

Jack graduated from the Columbus Academy in 1948, attended Colgate College and graduated from Ohio State in 1953. That same year he married Virginia Lape. Upon graduating from OSU he entered the Navy as an officer and was honorably discharged in 1955. Upon arriving back in Columbus he joined his father in the insurance business in the Beggs Building at 21 East State Street.

Like his father, Jack has served the community with pride and dignity. He is past president of the board of trustees of the Columbus Academy, Gladden Community House, University Club, the Golf Club and the insurance board of Columbus. With a long and distinguished career both in the insurance business and public service Jack is one of those individuals who have made Columbus a special place to live.

As a downtowner Jack vividly remembers going with his father to the open produce market on Town Street, especially to buy cheese from Isaly's. What a memory! He loved lunches at Paoletti's and Christmas Eve dinners at the University Club. Jack purchased suits from Harry Rook and John Pumphrey. He recounts renting his prom tuxedoes from Bob and Bo Gallo and later on buying clothing from Tom Lynch at Woodhouse Lynch.

Jack says he can still taste those great hamburgers at the Glass Bowl in Bexley. He also spent a great deal of time at the Toddle House on East Broad Street, Wentz's Drugstore soda fountain, Bexley Pharmacy, and Merkle's.

The Stephan's family contribution to both the insurance business and the community at large has helped Columbus grow and prosper. The Stephan name will forever be linked to community involvement in Columbus, Ohio.

Alan & Robert Weiler Jr.

Alan and Bob's parents were Robert and Elene. Robert Weiler Sr. moved to Columbus in 1913 when he was 13 years old. Mr. Weiler graduated from East High School followed by the Wharton School of Business at the University of Pennsylvania. In the early 1920's he worked for W.D. Zinn and Company who were in the commercial real estate business in downtown Columbus. They basically leased all of the space in downtown to the various business establishments.

In 1938, he bought into a property and casualty insurance agency. Mr. Weiler, who held both an insurance and real estate licenses died in 1976 following a tremendously successful career.

Alan - Alan entered the insurance business with the family firm in 1957 after completing his college years at Dartmouth and two years in the army. Alan and his entire family have always worked downtown. Their offices were at 175 South High Street, a stones throw south of Lazarus. Alan vividly remembers looking out of their fourth story window facing Lazarus and witnessing the hordes of people waiting to enter the store for "remnant days". He estimated that at 8:30am there would be five thousand people waiting for the store to open.

The main mode of traveling up and down High Street was street cars. Within a short distance from their offices were great eating establishments like the Sabre Lounge, Foresters, Mill's Cafeteria, Lazarus, Paoletti's and the Neil House. It was hard to go hungry in downtown Columbus in those days. Alan loved shopping at the Union where he once had a summer job in the luggage department during his high school years. That's when he decided that retailing was not for him. Growing up in Bexley, he loved the Glass Bowl and Town House Drive-In.

Today, Alan and his wife Bobbie enjoy semi-retirement by traveling and continuing their community affiliations. At any time Alan may have a joke or some yarn to spin and he will tell it to anyone who is willing to listen. Bobbie still enjoys a great game of tennis.

Bob Jr. - Bob and Missy met at the University of Arizona and moved back to Columbus in 1957. They have four children who all graduated from Eastmoor High School.

Bob's fulltime work has been devoted to real estate development and appraisals. Bob and his father leased downtown locations, representing the owners of the properties. During the 1950's and 1960's, they built homes in Whitehall and Bexley. In those days an expensive home in Bexley sold for around $40,000.

In 1960, Bob ventured into the appraisal business and throughout the years has created one of the most respected and admired appraisal companies in Central Ohio. In hindsight, Bob believes that downtown died with the opening of the Tuttle, Easton and Polaris shopping centers.

Initially, Lazarus resisted moving to the suburbs but the handwriting was on the wall. Shoppers were fleeing downtown and they needed to remain competitive. Once Lazarus opened branches surrounding I-270, downtown shopping died. Today, all shopping, including eating establishments, are freeway driven. When I asked Bob why downtown housing has not really grown he responded by saying that Columbus is not a "high rise" city but rather a horizontal city. It's our culture. In coming years it may change.

I also asked, "who were the visionaries of the 50's, 60's and 70's?" and he named four people:

- John McConnell
- Jack Nicklaus
- Mayor Sensenbrenner
- Les Wexner

Alan and Bob and their families are selfless in their contributions to the Columbus community. Each has served on numerous projects, boards and committees to help Columbus remain a thriving community. Their philanthropy is extraordinary and it once again proves that you win with people, especially special people like the Weilers.

Wing Yee

In the late 1920's, Walter Ming and George Yee were waiters in a Chinese restaurant on East State Street near the Ohio Theater. In 1930 they became partners and opened the Far East Restaurant in the location of the former Zettler's hardware store next to Paul's Food Market in Bexley. They couldn't obtain a liquor license in Bexley so they moved to their present location at 2801 East Main Street (now called Wing's) in 1941 and built a 12,000 square foot restaurant for $10,000.

In 1964 their partnership ended with Walter Ming staying and George Yee opening Yee's on East Broad Street (now known as Billy Lee's).

In 1966 the Far East closed its doors forever. It was sold and the new owners opened the Viking Steak House. It failed. Next opened a Mexican restaurant, Su Casa. It too failed. After both failures Wing Yee, George's nephew, felt that he could turn the old Far East back into a Chinese restaurant that would become successful again. Therefore, in 1970 he opened Wing's and it has remained a successful eastside establishment.

With his son Kenny, he has made Wing's an east side institution. Some say that Wing's bar is the best bar in Columbus. I know that every time I'm there the bar is packed with customers. Their single malt scotch collection is reputed to be one of the finest collections in the country.

Wing Yee, a Korean War veteran, is still the mainstay at the restaurant. A generation or two of eastsiders have passed through those hallowed doors and with Kenny and his dad at the helm it should go on forever.

If you don't enjoy Wing's and especially their veal cutlet, you just aren't a good American.

149

WHO COULD FORGET

Jim Ross	-	Salesman for Tom Carey
Dave Friedberg	-	Owner of Dunhill's
Jonas Rosenthal	-	Men's shoe salesman at Lazarus
Marvin Saylor	-	Salesman at Walker's
Robert J.G. Morton	-	Trust officer at City National Bank
Ike Cohen	-	Owner of Russell's Shoe Store
Tom Rice	-	Ran the trust department at City National Bank
Zelda Lasky	-	3rd floor Women's Better Coats at Lazarus
Insurance Legends	-	Chris Brush, Sam Chickerella, Bill Sayers, Red Oschner, Vern Miller, Sam Selby, Herman Tice, Herschel Stephan, Dick Wetherbee, Sam Loyer, Dennis Clark, Burt Holmes, Ralph Hoyer
Morry Tarcov	-	Men's clothing at The Union
M.E. Sensenbrenner	-	Passing out American flags to all of his "meets and greets"
Tom Kaplin/ Jim Petropolous	-	Played gin rummy every afternoon
Dick Wolfe	-	WBNS Radio & TV
Pete Halliday	-	Vercoe and Company
Vaudevillities	-	Since 1943
Vivian	-	Always at the organ at the Clarmont
James Rhodes	-	The Salesman Governor
Norman Folpe	-	Downtown Area Committee
Bob Marvin	-	Flippo the Clown
Spook Beckman	-	Started "Secret Santa" program
Lou Vierick	-	The florist
Bob & Mary Lazarus	-	Community involvement
Street Preacher	-	Always in front of Baker's Shoe Store
Jim Jacobs	-	City racquetball champion
Bill Engelman	-	Owner of the Continental
Ron Pizzuti	-	Began his career at Lazarus
Al Harmon	-	Pitchman on TV
Giant Don	-	TV commercials – jumped on mattresses
John McConnell	-	Blue Jackets guru
Guy Fracasso	-	Charm and wit
Gordon Campbell	-	Banker – Ohio National Bank
Les Wexner	-	Visionary
Dave Thomas	-	Hamburger flipper
John Galbreath	-	Kentucky Derby winner owner
Jim Trueman	-	Red Roof Inns
Sam Devine	-	Congressman

Nancy & Tad Jeffrey	-	Respected leaders
R.N. Larrimer	-	Worker's champion
Real Comfort	-	WBNS Radio salesman
Sumner F. Dennett	-	Headmaster – Columbus Academy
Esther Craw	-	The accordion lady at Deibel's
Jimmy Crum	-	"How about that sports fans?"
Chick Young	-	Camera store owner
John Kurgis	-	Wrestling's "Masked Marvel"
Kaye Kessler	-	Sports writer
Lou Berliner	-	Named a softball park for him
Harold Cooper	-	Baseball executive
Joseph Kinneary	-	Federal judge
Mel Schottenstein	-	Entrepreneurial lawyer
Fred Taylor	-	OSU Basketball coach
Troy Feibel	-	Sage attorney
Woody Hayes	-	Hung out at the Jai Lai
Gene Hammeroff	-	Advertising genius
Jack Nicklaus	-	18 major golf championships
Don Dunn	-	Indoor tennis facility
Eleanor Gelpi	-	Columbus Symphony supporter
Herbert Schiff	-	Shoe Corporation of America
Preston Wolfe	-	Publisher of the Columbus Dispatch
Gundy Lane	-	Lawyer and tennis buff
Earl Bradley	-	The Place Upstairs
Reverend Leon Troy	-	Revered community leader
Johnny Jones	-	Columnist
Harry Gilbert	-	Gilbert Shoes
Rabbi & Bessie Folkman		Temple Israel's immortal couple
Bill Westwater	-	Plumbing supplies
Barry Zacks	-	Max & Erma's
Jim & Babette Feibel	-	Advocates for families
Dave Levison	-	Pawnshop
Sig Munster	-	Legendary Columbus Academy athlete
Fred Shannon	-	Photographer – Columbus Dispatch
Maury Portman	-	President – Columbus City Council
Ben Zox	-	Cool lawyer
Al Cohen	-	Lazarus executive
Jimmy Goodman	-	Youthland
Michael Bloch	-	Meat man
Phale Hale Sr.	-	State of Ohio legislator
Dick Mann	-	Mann to man
Charles Y. Lazarus	-	My mentor
Jerry Lucas	-	All-time best OSU basketball player
Ted Hackett	-	Trust department – Huntington Bank

Jay Suitor	-	House beautiful
Dan Carmichael	-	Natural athlete
George Byers Sr.	-	Auto dealer
Richard Solove	-	Shopping centers
Nichols Vorys	-	OB/GYN
Sandy Solomon	-	OSU student landlord
Fred Simon	-	Safety director
Fred & Howard	-	German Village icons
Roger Garrett	-	The mighty Wurlitzer at the Ohio Theater
Byer & Bowman	-	Prestigious advertising agency
Lou Ferrigno	-	Bus boy at Jack Bowman's Steakhouse
Ken McClure	-	Mayor of Bexley
Elliott Grayson	-	York Steakhouses
Audrey Block	-	Hot bagels
Hal Block	-	Chopped liver
Jack Prather	-	Loan officer - Huntington
Wayne Brown	-	Big Bear
Simon and Haas	-	Necktie manufacturers
John Ziegler	-	Buckeye Letter Service
Norton Webster	-	Political strategist
Tom Benua	-	Men's clothing store
Bob Skuller	-	Luggage store
Al Haft	-	Haft Acres motel

Invariably, with any list, someone who should have been included will be left off. Please do me a favor, think of who else should not be forgotten and then they won't be. Thanks.

CREAM RISES TO THE TOP

Question…why do some business establishments last forever and others simply wither and die? Throughout this book I have recorded the history of some of the most famous business establishments Columbus has ever known. Marzetti's thrived for 87 years, Lazarus for over 120 years, Jeffrey Manufacturing Co. for 93 years, the Union 78 years, the Weiler Insurance and Real Estate companies and the Feinknopf Architectural firm for over 80 years and, of course, the Schoedinger Funeral Service which is still going and growing stronger since 1857.

In speaking with the Jeffreys, Lazaruses, Weilers, Madisons, Gundersheimers, Schoedingers, Levys, Feinknopfs and others I did find some common core values attributable to all of them. No matter if they were burying people, feeding them, or simply clothing them, these core values embraced:

1. They didn't have employees, they had associates.
2. Service was the by-word of their establishments.
3. If the customer got what he/she wanted, the business got what they wanted (profits).
4. Communication was face to face. No cell phones, faxes, computer e-mail or voicemail.
5. Always said "please" and "thank you."
6. Greeted all customers with a smile.
7. The customer was "KING".

In today's hectic world many business establishments have failed to grasp these important concepts developed years and years ago.

Visit any retail store at any mall and try to find a sales clerk. Ha! Perhaps Nordstroms is an exception. Call your cable company or telephone company with a service problem. Odds are it will take one hour or more of your time and you will eventually talk to a computer.

Unfortunately, the younger generation is immune to bad service. It doesn't seem to bother them as much as it bothers us "older folks." My generation, and that of my parents and grandparents, expected and received proper service and courtesies. They simply were in vogue. Today they are not expected therefore, few offer them.

With the natural ebb and flow of human behavior, the worm will turn and those attributes such as face to face communications, saying please and thank you and treating customers with reverence will return again. My hope is that I live long enough to see it.

WHERE DO WE GO FROM HERE?

In the late 1800's, the center of commerce was located around the produce market (Town and High). In the early 1900's it moved to Broad and High. In the 1960's it moved again to I-270.

I guess the burning question is-----why would people come back downtown to shop, to be entertained and to dine? Perhaps the only reason would be that they lived there. Currently, people go downtown for the following reasons:

- The symphony at the Ohio Theater
- Jazz Arts Group at the Southern Theater
- A play at The Palace Theater
- The Columbus Art Museum
- COSI
- A hockey game at Nationwide Arena
- A production at the Riffe Center
- Huntington Park (home of the Columbus Clippers)

Other than these reasons, downtown is non-existent in our minds.

I spoke with Tom Wentz, a leadership consultant, and asked him what will it take to revitalize downtown? His response was simple and direct, "You cannot revitalize something that has never been vitalized." He suggested that the proper question should be "what can be done to **transform** downtown Columbus into a vibrant city?"

Tom suggested to me that before you can have a strategy of what needs to be done, you first need a vision. One of Tom's visions would be to make downtown Columbus the home of the premier child healthcare center in the world.

I followed up that statement by asking what strategy he would employ to accomplish that lofty vision. He decided that is would all start with the City Center property. Instead of razing it at an estimated cost of fifteen to twenty million dollars, why not build a monorail to Children's Hospital. City Center could then be used for:

- Parking
- Parent housing
- Medical research
- Medical offices

All of this could be done at a cost of less than twenty million dollars. In addition, the monorail could be connected to the Arena District, OSU, the Short North, the fairgrounds, the Columbus Zoo, Bexley, Upper Arlington, Gahanna, Worthington, as well as to the airport.

As Children's Hospital continues to grow its reputation and prestige, more and more people will be drawn to the downtown area. With people come stores, entertainment and housing.

The current thought is to demolish City Center and turn it into a park. The park users will need police protection at the very time that city budgets are the tightest. It just doesn't make sense!

Until our community comes up with a viable vision, Sorry, downtown Columbus is closed.

As Bob Hope said so eloquently, "Thanks for the memories."

FINAL QUIZ

Where will the **"center"** of Columbus be located in fifty (50) years?

1. Broad and High Streets

2. The Arena District

3. The Brewery District

4. The Short North

5. Seventeenth and High

6. I-270

7. The outer outer belt

8. Children's Hospital

JUST SOME
FOOD FOR THOUGHT